Effective Business Intelligence with QuickSight

From data to actionable business insights using Amazon QuickSight!

Rajesh Nadipalli

BIRMINGHAM - MUMBAI

Effective Business Intelligence with QuickSight

First published: March 2017

Production reference: 1030317

Published by Packt Publishing Ltd.
Livery Place
35 Livery Street
Birmingham
B3 2PB, UK.

ISBN 978-1-78646-636-5

www.packtpub.com

Credits

Author

Rajesh Nadipalli

Reviewer

Arthur Zubarev

Commissioning Editor

David Barnes

Acquisition Editor

Ajith Menon

Content Development Editor

Aishwarya Pandere

Technical Editor

Dinesh Pawar

Copy Editors

Vikrant Phadkay
Safis Editing

Project Coordinator

Nidhi Joshi

Proofreader

Safis Editing

Indexer

Tejal Daruwale Soni

Graphics

Disha Haria

Production Coordinator

Aparna Bhagat

About the Author

Rajesh Nadipalli is currently Director, Professional Services and Support at Zaloni, an award-wining provider of enterprise data lake management solutions that enables global clients to innovate and leverage big data for business impact. Rajesh leads Hadoop-based technical proof-of-concepts, strategy, solution architectures, and post-sales product support for his clients. His clientele includes AIG, NBCU, Verizon, Du, American Express, Netapp, Dell-EMC, United Health Group, and Cisco. In his previous role as the director of product management, he was leading the product strategy, roadmap, and feature definitions for Zaloni's Hadoop data management platform.

Throughout his 20 plus years in IT, Rajesh has had a passion for data and held various roles as big data architect, solutions architect, database administrator (DBA), business intelligence architect, and ETL developer. He believes in using technology as a strategic advantage for his clients by improving productivity, performance, and real-time insight to relevant data.

Rajesh is also the author of *HDInsight Essentials*, by Packt publishing, which takes you through the journey of building a modern data lake architecture using HDInsight, a Hadoop-based service that allows you to successfully manage high volume and velocity data in Azure Cloud.

He is a regular blogger and his articles are published in Zaloni blog, Datafloq, and Dzone sites.

He holds a MBA from North Carolina State University and a BS in EE from University of Mumbai, India.

I would like to thank my family and friends for their love, support, and encouragement; and special thanks to my wife, Manasa, and daughter, Geetika, who were always there for support and inspiration.

About the Reviewer

Arthur Zubarev is a data platform engineer who specializes in developing fast data pipelines, data acquisition, analysis, validation, performance tuning, data warehousing, and visualizations. His skills and passion include relational and NoSQL database engines, big data, cloud technologies, streaming data, IoT, social web, and general programming.

Arthur is a data platform MVP for the sixth year, a member of the Data Advisors group for Microsoft, R for Visual Studio beta tester, MCDBA, MCAD, and MCITP. He strives to be an early adopter of new technologies and likes to embrace technical challenges. In addition, he is a frequent presenter and event organizer.

I would like to thank my wonderful family for always understanding the importance of my contributions to the technical community, even if that occurred at the expense of our spare time. This has allowed me to effectively deliver as much timely feedback as I could to produce this fantastic book.

www.PacktPub.com

For support files and downloads related to your book, please visit www.PacktPub.com.

Did you know that Packt offers eBook versions of every book published, with PDF and ePub files available? You can upgrade to the eBook version at www.PacktPub.com and as a print book customer, you are entitled to a discount on the eBook copy. Get in touch with us at service@packtpub.com for more details.

At www.PacktPub.com, you can also read a collection of free technical articles, sign up for a range of free newsletters and receive exclusive discounts and offers on Packt books and eBooks.

https://www.packtpub.com/mapt

Get the most in-demand software skills with Mapt. Mapt gives you full access to all Packt books and video courses, as well as industry-leading tools to help you plan your personal development and advance your career.

Why subscribe?

- Fully searchable across every book published by Packt
- Copy and paste, print, and bookmark content
- On demand and accessible via a web browser

Customer Feedback

Thanks for purchasing this Packt book. At Packt, quality is at the heart of our editorial process. To help us improve, please leave us an honest review on this book's Amazon page at `https://www.amazon.com/dp/1786466368`.

If you'd like to join our team of regular reviewers, you can e-mail us at `customerreviews@packtpub.com`. We award our regular reviewers with free eBooks and videos in exchange for their valuable feedback. Help us be relentless in improving our products!

Table of Contents

Preface

We live in an era where data defines business and is also growing exponentially, specifically in the cloud. Organizations that can empower their business with easy-to-use, fast, and real-time data will have a competitive edge over their peers; it is estimated that such organizations will save over $430 billion by 2020 compared to their peers.

Amazon QuickSight is an innovative next-generation cloud-powered BI service that makes it easy for anyone to build visualizations, perform ad hoc analysis, and quickly get business insights from their data. QuickSight delivers fast and responsive insights on big data and can scale to hundreds of users at a fraction of the cost when compared to traditional BI tools.

This practical example-rich guide begins by introducing you to Amazon QuickSight and reviewing what makes it unique, and explains how to get started building your first analysis on QuickSight. Moving ahead, you will get to know the entire AWS big data ecosystem, right from ingesting the data into various storage services and then use QuickSight's features to gain insights. We will next review how to perform lightweight transformations of the data within QuickSight in order to easily enrich your data and insights. Next, we will check out the various visualizations supported by QuickSight including analyses, dashboards, and story features that enable collaboration with your peers. We will next look at the QuickSight mobile application that empowers you with dashboards on the go. We will next look at how to build an end-to-end architecture for big data analytics using AWS Data Lake solution, which packages the most commonly needed components to jump-start such projects. Towards the end, you will learn what features the product is lacking and what's on the roadmap.

Throughout the book, you will be guided with step-by-step instructions, screenshots, data flow, and architecture models that you can reuse for your initiatives.

What this book covers

Chapter 1, *A Quick Start to QuickSight*, gives an overview of Amazon QuickSight and how it differs to traditional BI tools.

Chapter 2, *Exploring Any Data*, explains that QuickSight can analyze data from various sources including AWS data stores, files in common format, Salesforce, and popular database engines. QuickSight has a simple interface to connect to these sources and create datasets from them that can be stored in SPICE for subsequent analysis. In this chapter, we will first look at Amazon's big data ecosystem and then review how QuickSight can be used to connect to the various data stores.

Chapter 3, *SPICE up Your Data,* explores SPICE which is the accelerator of QuickSight, delivering interactive visualizations on large data sets in less than 60 seconds. SPICE is engineered with parallelism, automatic replications, and a rich calculation engine to serve thousands of users who can simultaneously perform fast interactive queries.

Chapter 4, *Intuitive Visualizations*, looks at visualization capabilities in detail. QuickSight can create a wide variety of visuals on different datasets imported to SPICE.

Chapter 5, *Secure Your Environment,* explains that to secure your BI environment you need to control which users have access to QuickSight and also what resources QuickSight has permissions to read.

Chapter 6, *QuickSight Mobile,* covers the QuickSight iOS mobile app. It allows you to stay connected to your data from anywhere, anytime, on your iPhone, iPad, or iPod touch. You can visualize, explore, and share your analyses, dashboards, and stories with an intuitive user experience and get answers to business questions in your palm.

Chapter 7, *Big Data Analytics Mini Project,* has a real-life use case leveraging the AWS Data Lake solution. Modern data architectures are moving to a data lake solution that has the ability to ingest data from various sources, transform, and analyze at big data scale. Amazon now offers a data lake solution that packages the most commonly needed big data components along with a web application to jump-start the data lake build out.

Chapter 8, *QuickSight Product Shortcomings,* covers some shortcomings of QuickSight. While the product is revolutionary and has a bold vision, there are several shortcomings in the current version for it to replace enterprise solutions, which are discussed in this final chapter.

What you need for this book

To follow the exercises in the book, you will need the following:

- Windows, Mac, or Linux laptop
- Register to Amazon QuickSight service in one of the tiers (Free/Standard/Enterprise)
- Optionally register for an AWS account for other services, such as S3, Athena, Redshift, RDS, Pipeline, and Data Lake solution

Who this book is for

This book is for all business professionals who have reporting, data analysis, and dashboard needs on a cloud-hosted Amazon service. It is also written for big data architects, enterprise architects, and business leaders involved in strategy who want to advance their organization's BI capabilities and improve overall business profitability.

Conventions

In this book, you will find a number of text styles that distinguish between different kinds of information. Here are some examples of these styles and an explanation of their meaning.

Code words in text, database table names, folder names, filenames, file extensions, pathnames, dummy URLs, user input, and Twitter handles are shown as follows: "For account name, type a unique name for your team, for example, `YourCompanyName-Marketing-Analytics`."

A block of code is set as follows:

```
{
  "Statement": [
    {
      "Action": [
        "iam:ListPolicyVersions",
        "iam:ListAccountAliases",
        "iam:AttachRolePolicy",
        "iam:GetPolicy",
      ]
    }
  ]
}
```

When we wish to draw your attention to a particular part of a code block, the relevant lines or items are set in bold:

```
{
  "Statement": [
    {
      "Action": [
        "iam:ListPolicyVersions",
        "iam:ListAccountAliases",
        "iam:AttachRolePolicy",
        "iam:GetPolicy",
      ]
    }
  ]
}
```

New terms and **important words** are shown in bold. Words that you see on the screen, for example, in menus or dialog boxes, appear in the text like this: "Next select the **STABBR** as the **Y axis** and **TUITFTE** as the **Value** field."

Warnings or important notes appear in a box like this.

Tips and tricks appear like this.

Reader feedback

Feedback from our readers is always welcome. Let us know what you think about this book-what you liked or disliked. Reader feedback is important for us as it helps us develop titles that you will really get the most out of. To send us general feedback, simply e-mail feedback@packtpub.com, and mention the book's title in the subject of your message. If there is a topic that you have expertise in and you are interested in either writing or contributing to a book, see our author guide at www.packtpub.com/authors.

Customer support

Now that you are the proud owner of a Packt book, we have a number of things to help you to get the most from your purchase.

Downloading the example code

You can download the example code files for this book from your account at `http://www.p acktpub.com`. If you purchased this book elsewhere, you can visit `http://www.packtpub.c om/support` and register to have the files e-mailed directly to you.

You can download the code files by following these steps:

1. Log in or register to our website using your e-mail address and password.
2. Hover the mouse pointer on the **SUPPORT** tab at the top.
3. Click on **Code Downloads & Errata**.
4. Enter the name of the book in the **Search** box.
5. Select the book for which you're looking to download the code files.
6. Choose from the drop-down menu where you purchased this book from.
7. Click on **Code Download**.

Once the file is downloaded, please make sure that you unzip or extract the folder using the latest version of:

- WinRAR / 7-Zip for Windows
- Zipeg / iZip / UnRarX for Mac
- 7-Zip / PeaZip for Linux

The code bundle for the book is also hosted on GitHub at `https://github.com/rnadipall i/quicksight`. We also have other code bundles from our rich catalog of books and videos available at `https://github.com/PacktPublishing/`. Check them out!

Downloading the color images of this book

We also provide you with a PDF file that has color images of the screenshots/diagrams used in this book. The color images will help you better understand the changes in the output. You can download this file from `https://www.packtpub.com/sites/default/files/down loads/EffectiveBusinessIntelligencewithQuickSight_ColorImages.pdf`.

Errata

Although we have taken every care to ensure the accuracy of our content, mistakes do happen. If you find a mistake in one of our books-maybe a mistake in the text or the code-we would be grateful if you could report this to us. By doing so, you can save other readers from frustration and help us improve subsequent versions of this book. If you find any errata, please report them by visiting `http://www.packtpub.com/submit-errata`, selecting your book, clicking on the **Errata Submission Form** link, and entering the details of your errata. Once your errata are verified, your submission will be accepted and the errata will be uploaded to our website or added to any list of existing errata under the Errata section of that title.

To view the previously submitted errata, go to `https://www.packtpub.com/books/content/support` and enter the name of the book in the search field. The required information will appear under the **Errata** section.

Piracy

Piracy of copyrighted material on the Internet is an ongoing problem across all media. At Packt, we take the protection of our copyright and licenses very seriously. If you come across any illegal copies of our works in any form on the Internet, please provide us with the location address or website name immediately so that we can pursue a remedy.

Please contact us at `copyright@packtpub.com` with a link to the suspected pirated material.

We appreciate your help in protecting our authors and our ability to bring you valuable content.

Questions

If you have a problem with any aspect of this book, you can contact us at `questions@packtpub.com`, and we will do our best to address the problem.

1
A Quick Start to QuickSight

We are in an era where data drives business and is also growing exponentially. The organizations that can empower their business with easy-to-use, fast, and real-time data will have the competitive edge over their peers. Amazon QuickSight is the next generation **Business Intelligence** (**BI**) application that can help you build interactive visualizations on top of various data sources hosted on Amazon Cloud Infrastructure. QuickSight delivers fast and responsive insights on big data and enables organizations to quickly democratize data visualizations and scale to hundreds of users at a fraction of the cost when compared to traditional BI tools.

In this introduction chapter, we will get an overview of Amazon QuickSight and its differences compared to traditional BI tools. We will cover the following topics:

- Era of big data
- Current BI landscape
- Rise of cloud powered BI
- Overview of QuickSight
- How is this different than other BI tools?
- High level architecture of a BI solution on QuickSight
- How does one get started with QuickSight?
- Performing your first analysis in under 60 seconds

Era of big data

We live in a digital era where data is generated everywhere, from smart connected devices to social media. In 2014, every second over 5,700 tweets were sent and 800 links were shared using Facebook, and the digital universe expanded by about 1.7 MB per minute for every person on earth (source: IDC 2014 report). This amount of data sharing and storing is unprecedented and is contributing to what is known as **big data**. In 2013, about 4.4 ZB were created and in 2020 the forecast is 44 ZB, which is 44 trillion GB (source: `http://www.emc.com/leadership/digital-universe/2014iview/executive-summary.htm`).

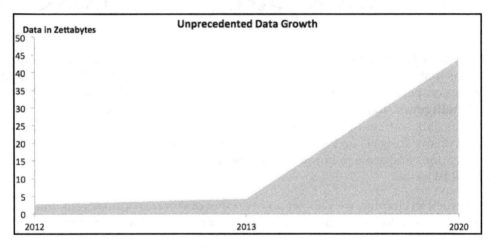

Figure 1.1: Data growth

IDC predicts that organizations that are able to analyze this big data and derive actionable insights will see an additional $430 billion in productivity benefits over their peers (source: *IDC FutureScape: Worldwide Big Data and Analytics 2016 Predictions*, `https://www.cloudera.com/content/dam/www/static/documents/analyst-reports/idc-futurescape.pdf`).

Let's look at some real use cases that have benefited from big data:

- IT systems in all major banks are constantly monitoring fraudulent activities and alerting customers within milliseconds. These systems apply complex business rules and analyze historical data, geography, type of vendor, and other parameters based on the customer to get accurate results and protect millions of customers across the globe.
- Commercial drones are transforming agriculture by analyzing real-time aerial images and identifying the problem areas. These drones are cheaper and more efficient than satellite imagery, as they fly under the clouds and can take images

anytime. They identify irrigation issues related to water, pests, or fungal infections, which thereby increases the crop productivity and quality. These drones are equipped with technology to capture high quality images every second and transfer them to a cloud-hosted big data system for further processing (you can refer to `http://www.technologyreview.com/featuredstory/526491/agricultural-drones/` for more information).

- Almost all shopping websites are using recommendation engines to improve customer experience like Amazon, Netflix, and Pandaro. These engines are sophisticated systems that perform big data analysis on historical buying preferences of the customer, ratings from social media, and associations rules from other similar customer purchases. This is now feasible due to advances in big data storage, compute, and in-memory analytics making these systems more intelligent and effective. You can refer to this article for more information at `http://www.sas.com/en_us/insights/articles/big-data/recommendation-systems.html`.

This unprecedented growth of data has resulted in need for faster insights, quicker co-relations, and the need to democratize data and analysis. Let's next look at the current BI landscape, key features they provide, and also their limitations.

Current BI landscape

Over the last 20 years, several vendors have built products to satisfy BI needs for organizations and this space is pretty crowded with big vendors and niche players that include Tableau desktop, Oracle OBIEE, SAP Business Objects, IBM Cognos, Qlick, and DOMO. Let's review the key features provided by the BI vendors.

Key features provided by BI tools

Most of the features offered by BI vendors fit into one of these categories:

- **Interactive reports**: It helps users to analyze data and support decision-making using slice-and-dice, drill down, trends, averages, percentile, and support ad hoc queries with ability to export data/charts.
- **Executive dashboards**: It presents data to business leaders in easy-to-understand **Key Performance Indicators (KPI)** and summary charts/tables. These dashboards are typically refreshed at regular intervals (weekly, monthly, or quarterly) based on the business need.

- **Integrations**: Integrates with various data sources to report stats on them and then publish results to websites, e-mails, and social media.
- **Metadata management**: It tracks the relationships between datasets, calculations, and hierarchies.

Typical process to build visualizations

Let's review the process for creating insights using traditional BI tools like Oracle OBIEE, SAP Business Objects, and IBM Cognos. At a high level, building a BI dashboard involves the following:

- Ingestion framework to collect data from source systems. These systems are typically files and relational databases.
- Standardize, clean, and build facts, dimensions, and aggregates based on key performance indicators requested by business.
- Build BI logical data models; typically star or snowflakes based on various dashboard needs.
- Build reports and dashboards on the web.
- Publish and share results with data analysts and business stakeholders.

The preceding data flow is shown in the following diagram and is primarily built by IT with regular consultation with data stewards and dashboard consumers:

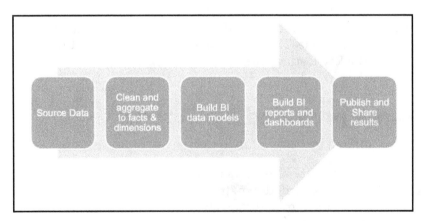

Figure 1.2: Process flow for traditional BI tools

Key issues with traditional BI tools

The traditional BI tools have primarily following issues that organizations are facing:

- BI software is expensive. In a study done by Amazon, a three year **Total Cost of Ownership** (**TCO**) is between $150 to $250 per user per month (source: AWS Summit Series 2016, Chicago at `https://aws.amazon.com/summits/chicago/`).
- It requires a large IT team to acquire data, model data, build reports, publish and repeat the entire process. A typical BI initiative will require at least 6 months before a production rollout of the dashboard (source: AWS Summit Series 2016, Chicago at `https://aws.amazon.com/summits/chicago/`).
- They do not work well with unstructured, NoSQL, and streaming data sources. The old BI tools often require ETL teams to build aggregate data in relational form to report.
- They do not scale well as data grows, which is required for big data analytics.
- They do not work well with cloud-hosted data sources like Amazon S3, RDS, and other cloud sources.

Rise of cloud BI services

There is an explosion of data being generated by cloud applications like `Salesforce.com`, Adobe Analytics, and HubSpot. In addition, enterprises are increasingly migrating their data to cloud with services like Dropbox, DocuSign, Google, AWS S3, and AWS RDS.

While enterprises have adopted **Software as a Service** (**SaaS**) for applications; the move to BI as a service has been slower. This trend is about to change and IDC predicts that by 2020, 50% of business analytics software will incorporate predictive analytics based on cloud platforms.

The definition of cloud BI would vary based on whom you talk to. First you have the traditional enterprise BI vendors; who have ability to host their software on a cloud server and call it a cloud service. Then you have the next generation BI vendors that have designed their software from ground up to use the elastic cloud services of Microsoft, AWS, and Google and offer real cloud BI service. AWS QuickSight falls under the second category of cloud BI vendors. Here are some of the popular cloud BI vendors Microsoft Power BI, Looker, Chartio, and Bime.

There are several operational and financial drivers that work in favor of cloud BI service, the key ones being:

- **Speed of implementation and deployment**: Infrastructure and software are available immediately provisioned exactly as required for the BI service
- **Elasticity**: Leveraging the compute power that can be scaled up or down on-demand based on business needs
- **Lower total cost of ownership**: It significantly reduces the infrastructure and related operational expenses
- **Improved connectivity**: For enterprises that already have moved to cloud for hosting their applications, the cloud BI is evolution and is the next step in their journey to be more cloud native

Next we will look into what makes AWS QuickSight stand out when compared to the others.

Overview of QuickSight

The Amazon web services team has been in the forefront of providing real solutions that are designed for massive scale; their S3 storage is the most popular cloud storage service and it is used by companies like Netflix, Nasdaq, Airbnb, and Redfin to name just a few. QuickSight is a new cloud BI service specifically designed to address the need for every day analytics and reporting. QuickSight allows enterprises to get started in minutes, access data from multiple sources, build interactive visuals, get answers fast, and tell a story with data.

While QuickSight has competitors, I believe it is poised to become the leader in cloud powered BI due to the deep connectivity to AWS services, next generation distributed architecture, with an in-memory caching layer on the worlds most scalable infrastructure. Additionally, AWS has made it extremely affordable that competitors will find it hard to match. Let's review in detail how QuickSight differs from other BI tools.

How is QuickSight different to other BI tools?

Amazon QuickSight was built to address pain points of the traditional BI tools and provides IT and business teams with a fast, cloud-powered BI service at one-tenth the cost of traditional BI software.

Here are the key features that make QuickSight the next generation cloud-powered BI tool:

- QuickSight empowers data analysts to build their reports quickly by pointing them to any data source without the need of a large IT team that traditionally has to build metadata in a BI tool before data analysts can use them.
- QuickSight pricing starts at $9 per user per month and is a complete managed service, which eliminates the need for software install and maintenance.
- QuickSight has deep integration within AWS data sources including RDS, DynamoDB, Kinesis, S3, Athena, and Redshift. It also supports user file uploads in Excel, CSV, TSV, and can also connect to Salesforce Cloud and on-premise databases. This list will continue to grow.
- QuickSight has smart visualizations that infer data type and provide suggestions for best possible visualizations. Additionally, QuickSight also suggests relationships between datasets.
- QuickSight has easy to use browser-based interface and does not require any desktop software to build metadata and/or reports.
- QuickSight has a special distributed and intelligent caching layer that provides blazing fast performance and response times.
- QuickSight allows users to share analysis, read only dashboards, and story board with peers.
- QuickSight has planned integration with a number of partner BI tools like Tibco, Domo, and Qlikview so that enterprises can leverage current investment, but still benefit from the caching and deep connectivity that QuickSight provides.

The following diagram shows the simplified flow from data to visuals using QuickSight:

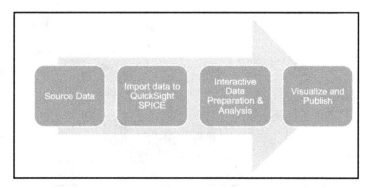

Figure 1.3: QuickSight simplified process

It has the following four steps, most of which can be done by a power user without the need for personal IT:

1. Source data from various sources including files, RDBMS on the AWS data platform.
2. Import data to QuickSight caching layer (SPICE).
3. Prepare/edit data if required for analysis.
4. Visualize and publish to dashboards.

High level BI solution architecture with QuickSight

Let's take a deeper look into how the complete solution architecture will look with QuickSight. The following diagram shows the high level architecture that takes data from various sources and presents as insights using QuickSight:

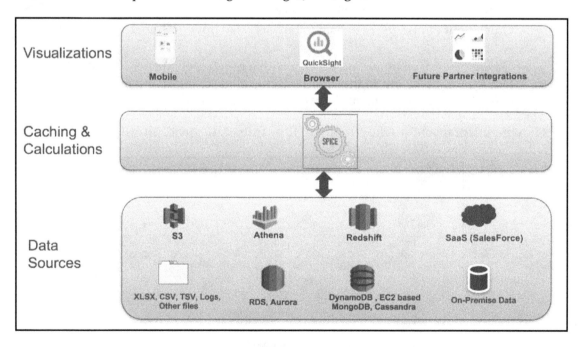

Figure 1.4: QuickSight architecture

Let's review this architecture starting from the bottom and going to the top:

- **Data Sources**: QuickSight can handle many data sources including files already in S3, files from your laptop in Excel files, standard log files, relational databases including RDS, Aurora, Redshift, DynamoDB, NoSQL databases, and on-premise databases. You can also connect to SaaS like Salesforce directly and report it on QuickSight.

- **Caching layer**: **Superfast, Parallel, In-memory, Calculation Engine** (**SPICE**) is an in-memory columnar database with a SQL-like interface that provides quick responses to the queries made by the visualization layer. SPICE has APIs and interfaces planned to integrate with partner products like TIBCO, Tableau, and DOMO.

- **Visualization**: QuickSight comes with intuitive visualizations with autographs based on automatic data type detection, native mobile user experience, and ability to integrate third-party visualization tools.

Next, let's look at how easy it is to get started and build a dashboard using QuickSight.

Getting started with QuickSight

In this section, we will review how to get started with QuickSight and build a real dashboard on data.

Registering for QuickSight

You have two options for signing up to QuickSight. If you are new to AWS, then sign up for Amazon QuickSight with a new AWS account to create an Amazon QuickSight account. If you have an existing AWS account and want to use IAM user credentials to create an Amazon QuickSight account, sign up for Amazon QuickSight with an existing account. Let's review each of these options in detail.

Signing up to QuickSight with a new AWS account

Let's review the steps to sign up to QuickSight with a new AWS account:

1. Go to `http://www.quicksight.aws` and choose **TRY IT FOR FREE**.
2. You will see a **Sign In or Create an AWS Account** page. Choose **I am a new user** and then follow the instructions to create a new account. This step involves receiving a phone call from the system.
3. After you are done signing up for an AWS account, you are taken to the Amazon QuickSight sign up page, where you specify an account name, an e-mail address for notifications about Amazon QuickSight, and a home AWS region. Here are a few guidelines for completing this form:
   - For account name, type a unique name for your team, for example, `YourCompanyName-Marketing-Analytics`. Account names can only contain characters (A-Z, or a-z), digits (0-9), and dashes (-).
   - For e-mail address, provide one where Amazon QuickSight should send service and usage notifications.
   - For the region, select the region closest to your physical location, and the same region where you have the majority of your other AWS resources (like Amazon RDS instances).
4. Click **Continue**.
5. Next, you will be redirected to **Grant Amazon QuickSight read-only access to AWS resources** page, accept the default selections to allow QuickSight to read from Amazon Redshift clusters, Amazon RDS instances, Amazon S3 buckets, and IAM entities you create under your AWS account.
6. Finally, click on **Finish** to complete your registration to Amazon QuickSight.

 You can next proceed to the *Building your first analysis in under 60 seconds* section.

Signing up to QuickSight with an existing AWS account

If you already have an AWS account, follow this section to create an Amazon QuickSight account that is connected to your AWS account. You can use your AWS credentials to login or use IAM user credentials.

To use IAM, the user must have a permissions policy attached that includes the following statements:

```
{
  "Statement": [
    {
      "Action": [
        "iam:ListPolicyVersions",
        "iam:ListAccountAliases",
        "iam:AttachRolePolicy",
        "iam:GetPolicy",
        "iam:GetPolicyVersion",
        "iam:CreateRole",
        "iam:CreatePolicy",
        "iam:CreatePolicyVersion",
        "iam:DeletePolicyVersion",
        "iam:GetRole",
        "iam:ListAttachedRolePolicies",
        "iam:ListRoles",
        "ds:CheckAlias",
        "ds:CreateIdentityPoolDirectory",
        "ds:CreateAlias",
        "ds:AuthorizeApplication",
        "ds:DescribeDirectories",
        "ds:UnauthorizeApplication",
        "ds:DeleteDirectory",
        "quicksight:Subscribe",
        "quicksight:Unsubscribe",
        "s3:ListAllMyBuckets"
      ],
      "Effect": "Allow",
      "Resource": [
        "*"
      ]
    }
  ],
  "Version": "2012-10-17"
}
```

Let's review the steps to sign up to QuickSight with an existing AWS account:

1. Go to http://www.quicksight.aws and choose **TRY IT FOR FREE**.
2. You will see a **Sign In or Create an AWS Account** page. Choose **I am returning user** and enter your username and password.

3. After you have signed up to your AWS account, you are taken to the Amazon QuickSight sign up page, where you specify an account name, an e-mail address for notifications about Amazon QuickSight, and a home AWS region. Here are a few guidelines for completing this form:

   - For account name, type a unique name for your team, for example, `YourCompanyName-Marketing-Analytics`. Account names can only contain characters (A-Z, or a-z), digits (0-9), and dashes (-).
   - For e-mail address, provide one where Amazon QuickSight should send service and usage notifications.
   - For the region, select the region closest to your physical location, and the same region where you have the majority of your other AWS resources (like Amazon RDS instances).

4. Click **Continue**.

5. Next, you will be redirected to **Grant Amazon QuickSight read-only access to AWS resources** page where the following is recommended:

   - Select the option for Amazon Redshift to allow QuickSight to auto-discover Redshift clusters associated with your AWS account.
   - Select the option for Amazon RDS to allow QuickSight to auto-discover RDS instances associated with your AWS account.
   - Leave IAM selected to allow QuickSight to get a list of IAM users associated with your AWS account. This will enable you to invite these users to access this Amazon QuickSight account.

6. Finally, click on **Finish** to complete your registration to Amazon QuickSight.

 You can now proceed to the, *Building your first analysis under 60 seconds* section.

Building your first analysis under 60 seconds

With QuickSight, it is really easy to build your analysis with minimal effort. Let's do a test drive of QuickSight and build our first analysis using data from the US Department of Education that provides information about college tuition across all the states in the USA.

Downloading data

The dataset is available from the following public URL:
`https://catalog.data.gov/dataset/college-scorecard`. Click on the **Download** icon as shown in the following screenshot to download raw data:

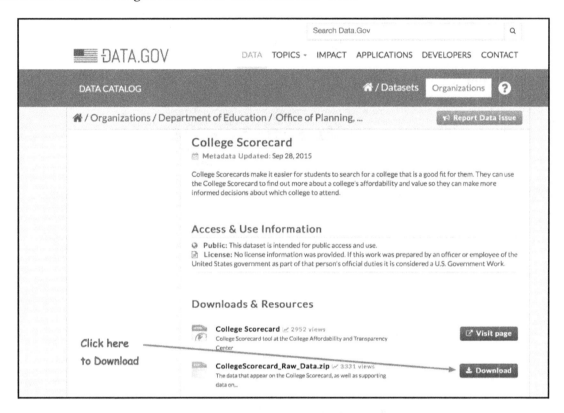

Figure 1.5: College scores raw data

Preparing data

The dataset has several files, one per each calendar year; for this demo, we will use the file `MERGED2013_PP.csv`. To simplify the analysis, I have selected a subset of the columns, changed all `NULL` to blank, changed `PrivacySuppressed` to blank, and uploaded this file to the following GitHub location:
`https://github.com/rnadipalli/quicksight/blob/master/sampledata/MERGED2013_PP.csv`.

QuickSight navigation

Once you have registered and started QuickSight you will see the home page. Let's review the key navigation icons that you need to get used to, as shown in the next screenshot:

- The **QuickSight** icon in the top-left is a quick way to get back to the home page
- To upload new data, click on **Manage data** in the top-right
- To create a new analysis, click on **New analysis** on the left-hand side below the QuickSight logo
- To manage your account settings, click on the person icon in the top-right corner

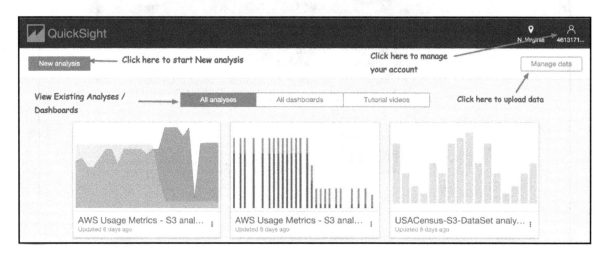

Figure 1.6: QuickSight navigation

Loading data to QuickSight

Let's explore the steps to load our data to QuickSight:

1. From the QuickSight home page, click on **Manage data** icon.
2. Next, click on the **New data set** icon and you will see **Create a Data Set** page with several options, as shown in the following screenshot. Select the **Upload a file** option and upload the MERGED2013_PP.csv file from your local desktop to AWS QuickSight:

Figure 1.7: Uploading a CSV file

3. After you have successfully uploaded the MERGED2013_PP.csv file, you will see a confirmation screen from QuickSight, as shown in the following screenshot. Click on the **Next** button to accept the defaults:

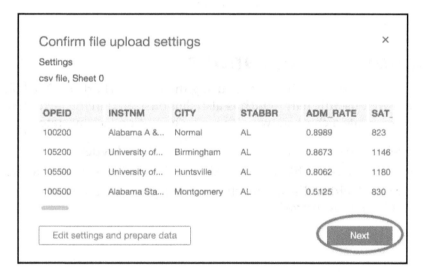

Figure 1.8: Confirm upload file settings

4. After the confirmation page, QuickSight imports the data to SPICE and provides quick access to visualization of the data, as shown in the following screenshot. Click on the **Visualize** button and then proceed to the next section:

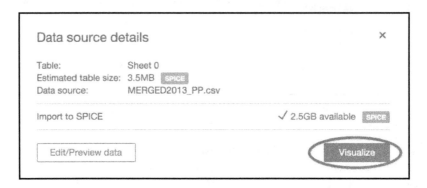

Figure 1.9: Data source details

Starting your visualizations

Now you are ready to start visualizing data using the built-in charts in QuickSight. Let's see how to create our first useful chart, which is also demonstrated in the next screenshot. Follow the steps to create a chart showing the average tuition fees by state:

1. First select the horizontal bar chart from the **Visual types**.
2. Next select the **STABBR** as the **Y axis** and **TUITFTE** as the **Value** field.
3. Next in the **Field wells** option, change the **Aggregate** type of the value from the default **Sum** to **Average**.

The visualization is complete, as shown in the following screenshot, and now you can explore the chart and get more insights from the data:

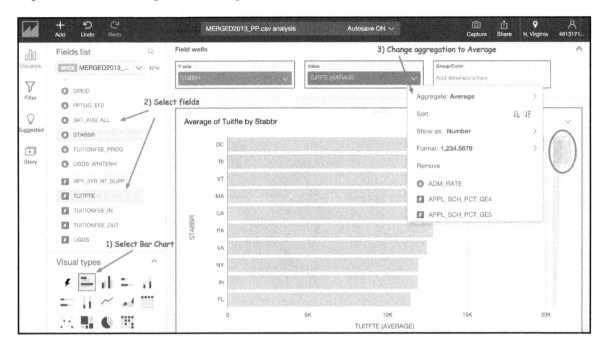

Figure 1.10: Bar chart

Building multiple visualizations

QuickSight additionally supports line graphs, area line charts, scatter plots, heat maps, pie graphs, tree maps, and pivot tables. You can next add another visual for the same dataset pretty easily and get further understanding of the data. In the following steps, we will see how to build a pie chart that shows the sum of in-state tuition by city:

1. Click on the **+** to add a new visual.
2. Select the pie chart from the **Visual types**.
3. Next select the **CITY** as the **Group/Color** and **TUTIONFEE_IN** as the **Value** field.
4. Notice the default aggregation for value is automatically set to **Sum**.

The visualization is complete, as shown in the following screenshot, and now you can explore the chart and get more insights from the data:

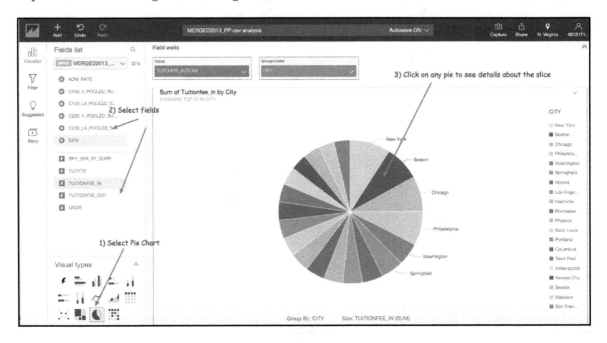

Figure 1.11: Pie chart

Summary

We live and breathe data with every action in our life, and organizations that have the ability to analyze relevant data in a timely manner will save an additional $430 billion by 2020 over their peers. While there is a need, the traditional BI platforms are slow, expensive, and are not designed to handle the volume, variety, and velocity needs that organizations face today.

Amazon QuickSight is the innovative and next-generation, cloud-hosted BI platform that addresses short falls of traditional BI systems and is at an extremely competitive price from $9 per user per month. QuickSight can source data from various sources including relational databases, files, streaming, and NoSQL databases. QuickSight also comes with an in-memory caching layer that can cache and calculate aggregates on the fly. With QuickSight, data analysts are truly empowered and can build intuitive reports in 60 seconds without any significant setup by IT. In the next chapter, we will look into the details of onboarding various data sources that are supported by QuickSight.

2
Exploring Any Data

QuickSight can analyze data from various sources including **Amazon Web Services** (**AWS**) data stores, files in common formats, Salesforce, and popular database engines. QuickSight has a simple interface to connect to these sources and create datasets from them that can be stored in SPICE for subsequent analysis. In this chapter, we will first look at Amazon's big data ecosystem and then review how QuickSight can be used to connect to the various data stores. The following topics will be covered:

- Amazon's big data ecosystem
- QuickSight-supported data sources
- QuickSight-supported data types and data sizes
- Use case review
- Uploading your own data from files, RDBMS, and SaaS to QuickSight
- Editing existing datasets
- Uploading data using Athena

AWS big data ecosystem

Amazon's big data ecosystem has several software services that enable business insights from data. These services can be broadly classified into four major categories - **Collect**, **Store**, **Analyze**, and **Orchestrate**, as shown in the following diagram:

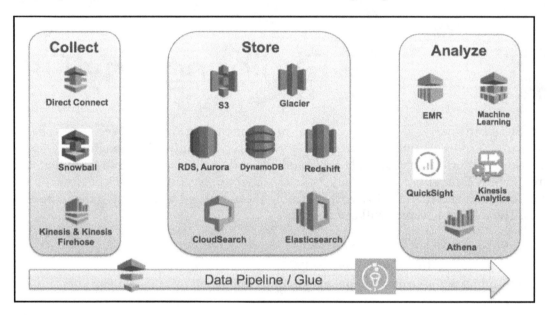

Figure 2.1: AWS big data ecosystem

Let's look at each category in detail.

Collect

The first step for any BI initiative is to collect data from external systems to Amazon for which AWS has the following services:

- **Direct connect**: With direct connect, you can establish private connectivity between AWS and your enterprise data center and provide an easy way to move data files from your applications to AWS for analysis
- **Snowball**: Snowball (also known as **Import/Export**) lets you import hundreds of terabytes of data quickly into AWS using Amazon-provided, secure appliances for secure transport

- **Kinesis and Kinesis Firehose**: Kinesis services enable building custom applications that process or analyze streaming data

Store

The data collected needs to be stored and Amazon offers several options, which you can pick and choose, based on latency and budget requirements. Following is a summary:

- **S3**: Amazon **Simple Storage Service** (S3) can be used to store and retrieve any amount of data. It is an object store and very reliable.
- **Glacier**: Glacier is an extremely low-cost storage service that provides secure, durable, and flexible storage for data backup and archival with low cost (1 cent per GB per month).
- **RDS and Aurora**: RDS services enables easy setup for the most commonly used relational databases in AWS including Oracle, MySQL, SQLServer, and Postgres and manages the time-consuming administration tasks of backup. The Aurora service is a MySQL compatible service at a fraction of the RDS cost.
- **Redshift**: The Redshift service provides a fast, full-managed data warehouse for a low cost ($1,000 per TB per year).

Analyze

Once data is in Amazon, we have several options to analyze data. Following is a summary:

- **EMR**: Amazon EMR provides a managed Hadoop framework that makes it an easy, fast, and cost-effective way to process a vast amount of data at scale and on-demand.
- **Machine learning**: Machine learning provides visualization tools and wizards for creating machine learning models and execute them on your big data.
- **QuickSight**: QuickSight is the fast, cloud-powered BI service and the theme of this book.
- **Athena**: It is a query service that makes it easy to analyze data directly from files in S3 using standard SQL statements. Athena is server-less, which makes it really stand out since there is no additional infrastructure to be provisioned.

Orchestrate

To move, orchestrate, and integrate data between the various AWS stores, Amazon has two key products; Data Pipeline and Glue. The following is a summary of these products:

- **Data Pipeline**: Amazon Data Pipeline allows reliable data movement from different AWS compute and storage services, as well as on-premise data sources at specified intervals.
- **Glue**: Glue is a fully managed ETL service (launched Dec 2016) with a data catalog. It crawls data sources, identifies data formats, allows transformations to be built using an IDE, and schedules these jobs.

This completes the AWS big data ecosystem overview. Next, let's look at how to onboard data to QuickSight in detail.

Supported data sources

QuickSight supports broadly three types of data sources: relational, file, and SaaS. For relational sources it supports Athena, RDS, Redshift, MySQL, and SQL Server sources. For file sources, it supports Excel, CSV, and common log formats in S3. For SaaS it supports Salesforce.

Before we explore data sources, I would like the readers to get familiar with QuickSight concept of data source and dataset. A data source identifies sources like relational database, S3 filesystem, and SaaS system like SAP. A dataset identifies specific data in a data source, for example, a table is a dataset in a RDBMS data source. A dataset is imported into SPICE for fast access.

Now let's explore the list of supported data sources using the following steps:

1. From the QuickSight home page click on **Manage data**, which will show a list of existing datasets and a summary of your current SPICE utilization, as shown in the following screenshot:

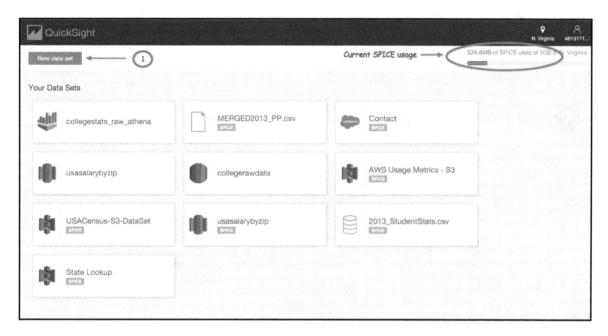

Figure 2.2: Adding a new dataset

2. Next from this page (**Manage data**), click on **New data set** to see the list of sources that QuickSight can connect to, as shown in the following screenshot:

Figure 2.3: Supported datasets

Let's review this list of data sources in detail:

- Files you can upload from your laptop in common formats that is, delimited (.csv, .tsv), log files (.clf), extended log files (.elf), and Excel (.xlsx).
- Salesforce cloud instance.
- Files in S3, that is, delimited (.csv, .tsv), log files (.clf), and extended log files (.elf). S3 also supports compressed files if .gzip is used; for other compressed formats, you will need to decompress first before importing them.
- Athena service that allows SQL queries on S3.
- RDS instances for MySQL (any version), PostgreSQL (any version), and Microsoft SQL Server 2012. You can source from any table and in case of PostgreSQL, the materialized view is also supported.
- Redshift cluster.
- Redshift external account.
- MySQL in Amazon EC2, on your local network or in some other Internet accessible environment.

- PostgreSQL in Amazon EC2, on your local network or in some other Internet accessible environment.
- SQL Server in Amazon EC2, on your local network or in some other Internet accessible environment.
- Aurora service provides MySQL or PostgresSQL compatible databases at lower cost and improved performance than the standard open source databases.
- MariaDB in Amazon EC2, on your local network or in some other Internet accessible environment.

Supported data types

QuickSight supports the following primitive data types: date, float, integer, and string. If you load data from files and/or databases that contain fields that cannot be implicitly converted to the preceding primitive data types, ensure that they are explicitly converted before they are imported to QuickSight. The following table lists the source data types for specific database engines:

Database type	Numeric data types	String data types	Date-time data types	Boolean data types
SQL Server	Bigint Decimal Float Int Money Numeric Real Smallint Smallmoney Tinyint	Char Nchar Nvarchar Text Varchar	Date Datetime Datetime2 Datetimeoffset Smalldatetime	bit
Aurora, MariaDB, and MySQL	Bigint Decimal Float Int Integer mediumint numeric Smallint Tinyint	Binary Blob Char Enum Set Text Varbinary Varchar	Date Datetime Timestamp Year	Tinyint

PostgreSQL	Bigint Decimal Double Integer Numeric Precision Real Smallint	Char Character Varchar Varying character Text	Date Timestamp	Boolean
Athena	Bigint Decimal Double Integer Real Smallint Tinyint	Char Varchar	Date Timestamp	Boolean

The `Datetime` field should be in one of the following formats, which are based on the Joda project class `DateTimeFormat` (http://www.joda.org/joda-time/apidocs/org/joda/time/format/DateTimeFormat.html):

- `yyyy-MM-dd`, for example, `2016-10-01`
- `yyyy-MM-ddTHH`, for example, `2016-10-01T16`
- `yyyy-MM-ddTHH:mm`, for example, `2016-10-01T16:08`
- `yyyy-MM-ddTHH:mm:ss`, for example, `2016-10-01T16:08:29`
- `yyyy-MM-ddTHH:mm:ss.SSS`, for example, `2016-10-01T16:08:29.322`
- `yyyy-MM-ddTHH:mm:ss,SSS`, for example, `2016-10-01T16:08:29, 322`
- `yyyy-MM`, for example, `2016-10`
- `yyyy-MM-ddTHH:mm:ss.SSSZZ`, for example, `2016-10-01T16:08:29.322-08:00`
- `yyyy-MM-ddTHH:mm:ss,SSSZZ`, for example, `2016-10-01T16:08:29,322-08:00`
- `yyyy-MM-ddTHH:mm:ssZZ`, for example, `2016-10-01T16:08:29-08:00`
- `yyyy-DDD`, for example, `2016-066`
- `yyyy-DDDTHH:mm:ss.SSSZZ`, for example, `2016-066T16:08:29.322-08:00`
- `yyyy-DDDTHH:mm:ssZZ`, for example, `2016-066T16:08:29-08:00`
- `yyyy-MM-dd HH:mm:ss.SSS`, for example, `2016-10-01 16:08:29,322`

- yyyy-MM-dd HH:mm:ss, for example, 2016-10-01 16:08:29
- yyyyMMdd, for example, 20161001
- yyyyMMddTHHmmss.SSSZ, for example, 20161001T160829.322-0800
- yyyyMMddTHHmmssZ, for example, 20161001T160829-0800
- yyyyDDD, for example, 2016066
- yyyyDDDTHHmmss.SSSZ, for example, 2016066T160829.322-0800
- yyyyDDDTHHmmssZ, for example, 2016066T160829-0800
- yyyy, for example, 2016
- yyyy/MM/dd HH:mm:ss, for example, 2016/10/01 16:08:29
- yyyy/MM/dd, for example, 2016/10/01
- MM/dd/yyyy, for example, 10/01/2016
- MM/dd/yy, for example, 10/01/15
- M/d/yyyy, for example, 1/1/2016
- M/d/yy, for example, 1/1/15
- MM/dd/yyyy HH:mm:ss, for example, 10/01/2016 16:08:29
- MM/dd/yy h:mm a, for example, 10/01/15 4:08 PM
- MM/dd/yy HH:mm:ss, for example, 10/01/15 16:08:29
- MM/dd/yy HH:mm, for example, 10/01/15 16:08
- MM/dd/yy hh:mm a, for example, 10/01/15 04:08 PM
- MMM dd, for example, Oct 01
- MMM dd yyyy HH:mm:ss, for example, Oct 01 2016 16:08:29

Supported data sizes

Amazon QuickSight uses SPICE in-memory caching and hence there are some limits to data from files and tables. You can see the amount of SPICE you are using by clicking on **Manage data** in the top-right corner. Now let's look at the file and table limits in detail.

File limits

Any single file uploaded to QuickSight directly or from S3 must be 1 GB or less. If multiple files are imported from S3, the total size of files specified in the manifest file must be less than 5 GB and the total number of files should not exceed 100. The number of columns in a file should not exceed 200 and the number of characters per row should be less than 25,400.

Table limits

Any table or query result set imported into SPICE must be less than 10 GB. If you are dealing with tables with larger datasets, use filters to reduce the number of records to analyze. Data in any string column must be 511 characters or less.

Use case review

For the next few chapters, let's bring in a real-life use case and see how QuickSight can help. For this use case, we will analyze college ratings from the Department of Education (https://www.ed.gov) and combine information from Census. The following diagram shows the overall data intake flow. In the subsequent sections, I will go into detail on each of the individual data intake processes:

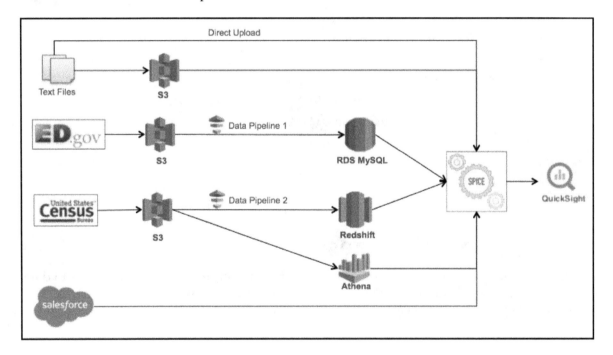

Figure 2.4: Use case data sources

Next, we will look into loading data from these various sources to QuickSight.

Permissions on AWS resources

Before we get started on loading data from the various sources, we first need to grant permissions to QuickSight to access your AWS resources. Follow these steps to grant access:

1. From the QuickSight home page, select **Manage QuickSight**.
2. Click on **Account settings** on the left-hand side menu.
3. Click on **Edit AWS permissions** as follows:

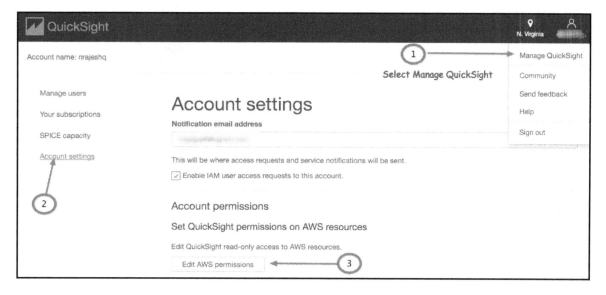

Figure 2.5: AWS account permissions

4. This will show the **Edit QuickSight read-only access to AWS resources**, as shown in the next screenshot. From here you can grant/revoke access to QuickSight from Redshift, RDS, S3, and Athena sources. After you make changes, do remember to click on **Apply**.

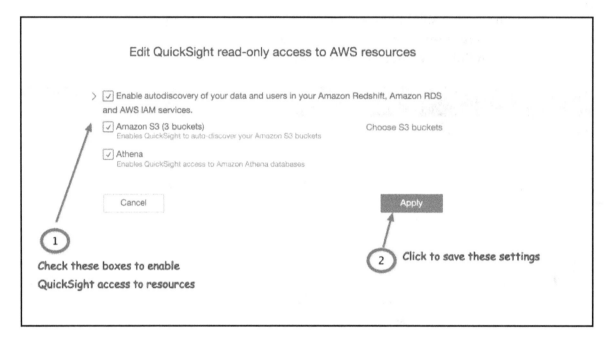

Figure 2.6: Grant access to all sources

Now we can start loading data from various sources and create new datasets in QuickSight.

Loading text files to QuickSight

The easiest way to load data to QuickSight is to just upload it to SPICE, which was explained in Chapter 1, *A Quick Start to QuickSight*. Another alternative to uploading text files is to use S3 storage and this section will detail this flow.

Uploading a data file to S3

For this demonstration, we will use the file `USAStateAbbr.csv`, which has a list of USA state codes and the corresponding full names.

 The sample files are in GitHub at `https://github.com/rnadipalli/Quic kSight/tree/master/sampledata`.

Here are the detailed steps to upload a file to an S3 filesystem:

1. Download the file to your local system (laptop).
2. Upload the file to AWS S3, login to our account, and from the **Services** menu select **S3**.
3. Select the S3 bucket or create a new S3 bucket. In the next screenshot, I have selected the `collegescorecard` bucket that I created earlier.
4. Click on the **Upload** button, select the local file from your system, and then upload.

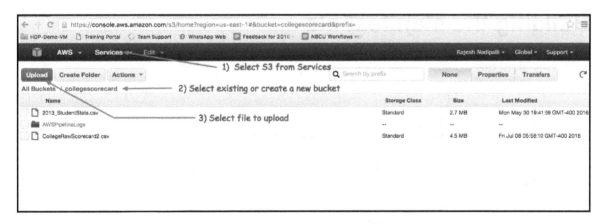

Figure 2.7: Upload text file to S3

5. Now that the file is uploaded to S3; review its properties, which will be needed in later steps, as shown in the following screenshot:

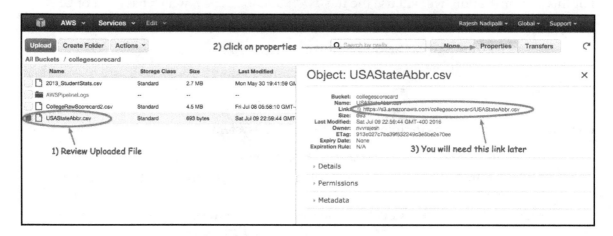

Figure 2.8: S3 file properties

Building the manifest file

To upload files to SPICE, we first need to create a manifest file, which is a JSON file with the following structure:

```
{
  "fileLocations": [
    {"URIs": ["uri1", "uri2", "uri3"]},
    {"URIPrefixes": ["prefix1", "prefix2", "prefix3"]}
  ],
  "globalUploadSettings": {
    "format": "CSV",
    "delimiter": ",",
    "textqualifier": "'",
    "containsHeader": "true"
  }
}
```

The manifest file elements are described as follows:

- `fileLocations`: This is used to specify the files to be uploaded. You can specify a list of file `URIs` in an array or specify `URIPrefixes` where all files in the specific folder will be imported. QuickSight does not recursively retrieve files from child folders.
- `globalUploadSettings` (optional): This is used to specify `format`, `delimiter`, `textqualifier`, and `containsHeader`.

The following is the manifest example to load the `USAStateAbbr` file:

```
{
  "fileLocations": [
    {
      "URIs": [
        "https://s3.amazonaws.com/collegescorecard/USAStateAbbr.csv"
      ]
    }
  ],
  "globalUploadSettings": {
    "format": "CSV",
    "delimiter": ",",
    "containsHeader": "true"
  }
}
```

Creating a new QuickSight dataset from S3

Next, we will see how this file can be imported to QuickSight using the following steps:

1. From the QuickSight home page, click on **Manage data**.

2. Next, select **New data set** and then select **S3**. Next, upload the manifest file created in the previous steps and click on **Connect**, as shown in the following screenshot:

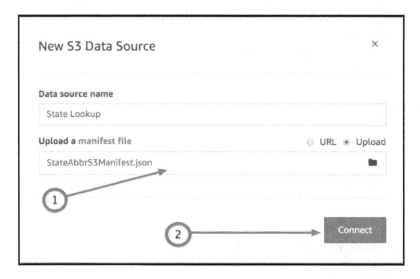

Figure 2.9: New S3 dataset

This completes the import of S3 data as a dataset in QuickSight that can be further visualized for analysis.

Loading MySQL data to QuickSight using the AWS pipeline

In this section, we will look into the data flow path from `https://www.ed.gov/` to QuickSight that uses a MySQL database. The source data is obtained from the public site and provides information about colleges in the USA.

The path to get to QuickSight involves the following steps:

1. Uploading data to S3.
2. Creating an AWS Data Pipeline to load data from S3 to MySQL.
3. Loading data from MySQL to QuickSight.

Pre-requisites

The following are the pre-requisites to load data from MySQL to QuickSight:

- Must have an RDS instance created. In this example, I will show an RDS MySQL instance.
- Data file must be CSV. It should not contain any header rows.
- You must have a database username and password that can connect to the database from QuickSight with the SELECT permission on some system tables so that QuickSight can estimate the table size. The following table identifies the system tables that the user account needs permission to select:

Database type	Access needed for tables
MySQL	INFORMATION_SCHEMA.STATISTICS INFORMATION_SCHEMA.TABLES
PostgreSQL	pg_stats pg_class pg_namespace

Uploading data to S3

From the public site, download the data file to your local system and upload to S3. This process is the same as described in the *Loading text files to QuickSight* section. Website link: `https://catalog.data.gov/dataset/college-scorecard`.

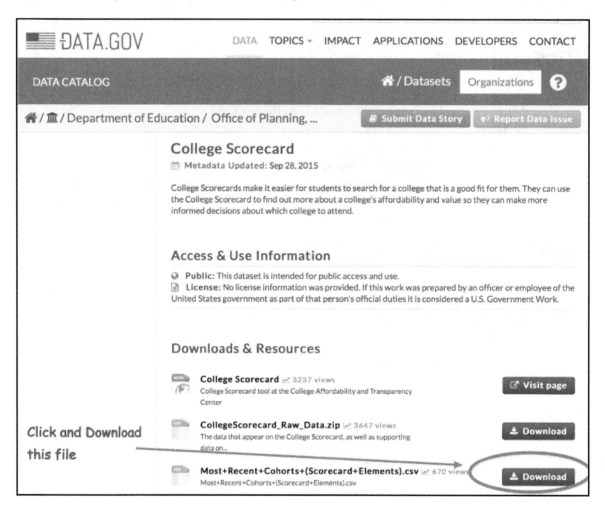

Figure 2.10: College scorecard data (data.gov)

Creating and executing the AWS Data Pipeline

Next, to load the data from S3 to an RDS MySQL instance, we will use the AWS Data Pipeline service, which makes it easy to build ETL pipelines with a web interface. From the **Services** list, click on **Data Pipeline**, and then, click on **Create new pipeline**, as shown in the following screenshot:

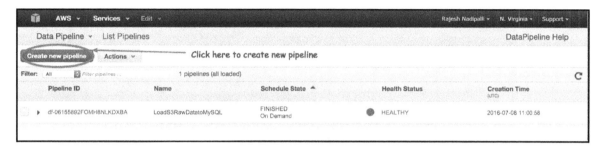

Figure 2.11: AWS pipeline creation

The next screenshot shows the **Create Pipeline** form, enter the details as follows:

- **Name** and **Description**: Provide an appropriate name and description (optional).
- **Source**: Select from the drop-down menu, **Load S3 data into RDS MySQL table**.

- **Parameters**: Provide the appropriate MySQL credentials, S3 location, insert query, MySQL table name, and the create table query.

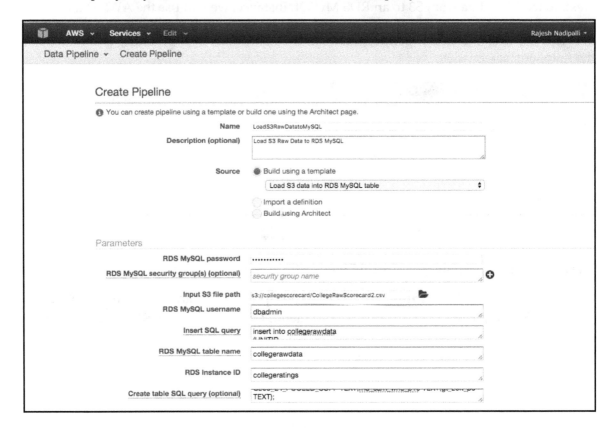

Figure 2.12: Load S3 to MySQL pipeline

 For reference, you can import the pipeline that I have saved in GitHub at this location: `https://github.com/rnadipalli/QuickSight/blob/maste r/awsdatapipelines/LoadS3toMySQLPipeline.json`.

- Next, provide schedule information or click on **Activate** to kick off the pipeline, as shown in the following screenshot:

Figure 2.13: Load S3 to MySQL pipeline schedule

- Optionally, you can view the pipeline in a graphical form if you click on **Edit in Architect** as follows:

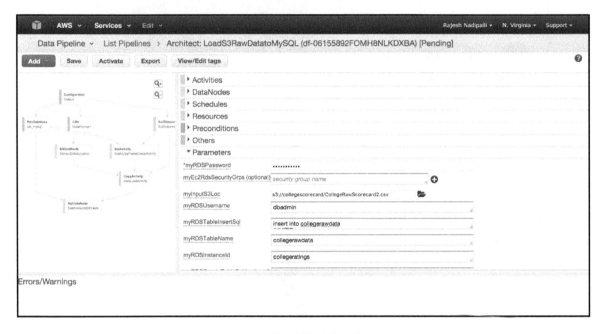

Figure 2.14: S3 to MySQL pipeline architect

- AWS will now execute this pipeline on an EC2 instance that you have specified at configuration. The following screenshot shows the monitoring page. If the execution has any failures, you can click on details to view the error message.

Figure 2.15: Pipeline execution

Creating a new QuickSight dataset from MySQL

Now that data is in the RDS MySQL instance, follow these steps to create a new dataset in QuickSight:

1. From the QuickSight home page, click on **Manage data**.
2. Next, select **New data set** and then select **RDS** option.
3. Next, enter details of the RDS data source, as shown in the following screenshot, and then click on **Connect**:

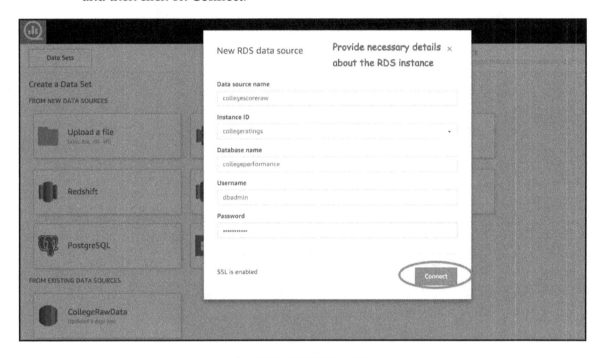

Figure 2.16: Load RDS MySQL to SPICE

4. You will next get a list of tables for that database. Select the table where data was just imported to `collegerawdata`, as shown in the following screenshot:

Figure 2.17: MySQL state dimension

5. Next, you have the option to prepare the data or straight import to SPICE and visualize it in QuickSight, as seen in the following screenshot:

Figure 2.18: MySQL RDS data confirmation

This completes the loading of data from MySQL to QuickSight.

Loading Redshift data to QuickSight

In this section, we will look into the data flow path from the US census to QuickSight using a Redshift data store. The source data is obtained from the public site and provides information about household income and population in the USA by zip code. The path to get to QuickSight involves the following steps:

1. Uploading data to S3.
2. Creating an AWS Data Pipeline to load data from S3 to Redshift.
3. Loading data from Redshift to QuickSight.

Pre-requisites

The following are the pre-requisites to load data from Redshift to QuickSight:

- Must have a Redshift instance created.
- Data file must be a CSV. It cannot contain a header in the data file.
- You must have a database username and password that can connect to the database from QuickSight with the SELECT permission on some system tables so that QuickSight can estimate the table size. These tables are pg_stats, pg_class, and pg_namespace.

Uploading data to S3

For this demonstration, we will use the file `USACensusSalarybyZip.csv` which has median and mean household salary by zip code. This will help us understand if the college tuition fees are affordable by the local residents. The source for this data is from the University of Michigan, Population Studies Center website, which gets this from the Census Bureau (`http://www.psc.isr.umich.edu/dis/census/Features/tract2zip/`).

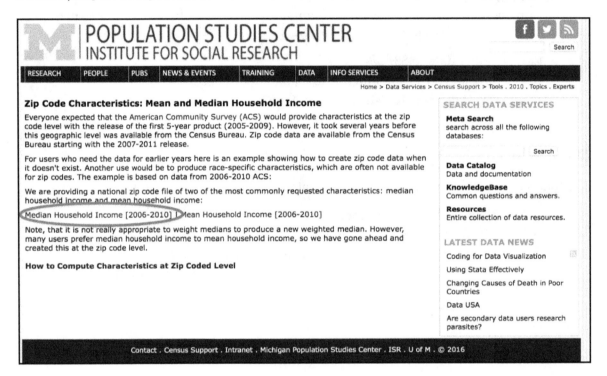

Figure 2.19: University of Michigan Census site

The preceding screenshot shows the University of Michigan Population Studies Center web page with the download link highlighted.

 The sample files are also in GitHub (edited and removed header line and converted text to number) `https://github.com/rnadipalli/QuickSight /tree/master/sampledata`.

Here are the detailed steps to upload a file to an S3 filesystem:

1. Download the file to your local system (laptop).
2. Next, to upload the file to AWS S3, login to your account and from the **Services** menu, select **S3**.
3. Next, select the S3 bucket or create a new S3 bucket. For this file I have selected `collegescorecard` bucket that I created earlier.
4. Next click on the **Upload** button, select the local file from your system, and then upload.

This completes the upload of the `USACensusSalarybyZip.csv` file to S3.

Creating and executing an AWS Data Pipeline

Next, to load the data from S3 to a Redshift instance, we will use the AWS Data Pipeline service. From the **Services** list, click on **Data Pipeline** and then click on **Create new pipeline**.

The next screenshot shows the **Create Pipeline** form, enter the details as follows:

- **Name** and **Description**: Provide an appropriate name and description.
- **Source**: Select from the drop-down menu; **Load data from S3 into Redshift**.

- **Parameters**: Provide the appropriate Redshift credentials, S3 location, insert query, table name, and the create table query. The table has the following structure: `zip varchar(20)`, `medianincome int`, `meanincome int`, `populationcount int`.

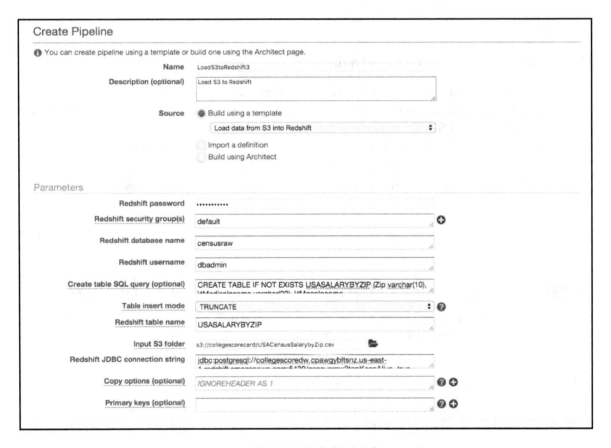

Figure 2.20: AWS pipeline for S3 to Redshift

- Next, provide schedule information or click on **Activate** now to kick off the pipeline now.

For reference, you can import the pipeline I have saved in GitHub at this location: `https://github.com/rnadipalli/QuickSight/blob/master/awsdatapipelines/LoadS3SalarytoRedshiftPipeline.json`.

- AWS will now execute this pipeline on an EC2 instance that you have specified at configuration and the data is published to a Redshift database.

Creating a new QuickSight dataset from Redshift

Now that data is in the Redshift instance, follow these steps to load it to SPICE:

1. From the QuickSight home page, click on **Manage data**.
2. Select **New data set** and then select **Redshift** option.
3. Enter details of the Redshift data source, as shown in the following screenshot, then and click on **Connect**:

Figure 2.21 Load Redshift to SPICE

4. Next select the schema and table from the drop-down menu, as shown in the following screenshot:

Figure 2.22 Redshift table selection

5. Select **Prepare data** to edit the data format, as shown in the following screenshot:

Figure 2.23: Redshift prepare data

6. In the **Prepare** screen, you can see all the fields and data; next, click on **Prepare data & visualize** to analyze this data in QuickSight.

Figure 2.24: Dataset preview

7. Now in QuickSight visualization, you can change the visualization type, dimensions, measures, and see an interesting scatterplot that shows which zip codes have the highest average median income and the corresponding population. With our dataset, zip code 21771 has a population of 26,023 and average median salary of $105,144.

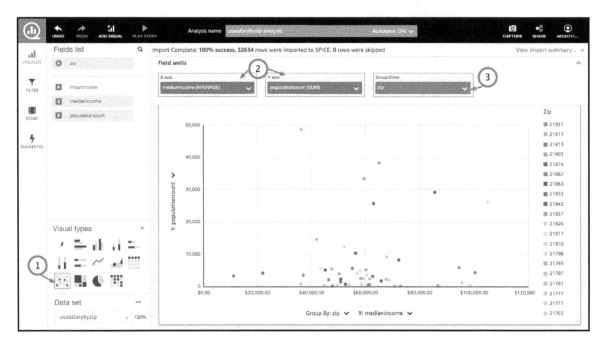

Figure 2.25: Redshift data visualization

Loading data from Athena to QuickSight

In this section, we will review how to use Athena, which is a new service from Amazon that enables SQL queries on S3 files without the need for any additional infrastructure.

Uploading data to S3

For this demonstration, we will use all of the files for CollegeScorecard from Data.gov as discussed in Chapter 1, *A Quick Start to QuickSight, Building your first analysis under 60 seconds* section.

The dataset is available from the following public URL https://catalog. data.gov/dataset/college-scorecard.

Here are the detailed steps to upload a file to an S3 filesystem:

1. Download the CollegeScorecard_Raw_Data.zip to your local system (laptop) and unzip the file.
2. To upload the file to AWS S3, login to our account and from the **Services** menu, select **S3**.
3. Select the S3 bucket or create a new S3 bucket. In the following screenshot, I have selected the collegescorecard bucket that I created earlier.
4. Create a folder CollegeRaw and then subfolders, one for each year 2010, 2011, 2012, and 2013, as shown in the following screenshot:

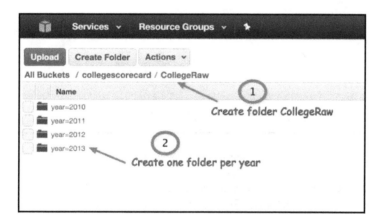

Figure 2.26: Athena S3 upload

5. To each subfolder, upload the corresponding data file; for example, MERGED2010_PP.csv file goes to year=2010 subfolder and repeat the same for all years.

This completes the data loading to S3 and next we will see how to view this data in Athena.

Creating a table in Athena

Now that the data is loaded into S3, we can query it using Athena with the following steps:

1. Open the AWS management console for Athena using this link
    `https://console.aws.amazon.com/athena/home` OR search for Athena in the
    AWS services search bar.

2. Using the **Query Editor**, run the `create database` statement, as shown in the
    following screenshot:

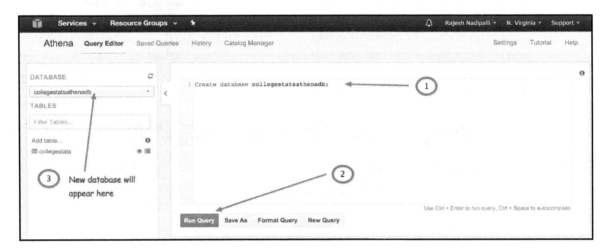

Figure 2.27: Athena create database

3. The new database, `collegestatsathenadb`, should appear in the drop-down
    menu on the left-hand side. Select the new database.

4. Create a new table for the files in S3 on the `collegescorecard` raw data with a partition clause. The query is in GitHub at this location: `https://github.com/rnadipalli/quicksight/blob/master/sqlscripts/loadto Athena.sql`.

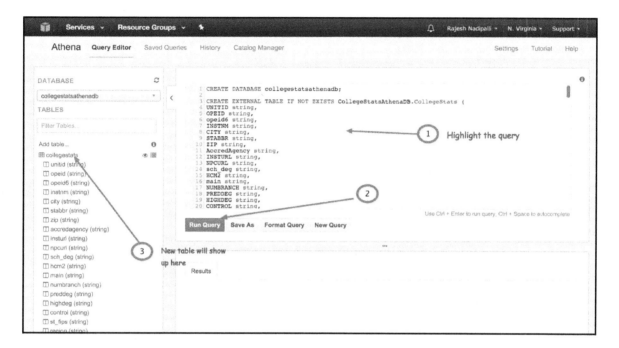

Figure 2.28: Athena create table

5. After the table is created, verify it by browsing it on the left-hand panel.

6. To load all partitions of the table, run the following command:

```
MSCK REPAIR TABLE CollegeStatsAthenaDB.CollegeStats;
```

7. You can now query the table with `select * from CollegeStatsAthenaDB.CollegeStats limit 5;` and view data as shown in the following screenshot:

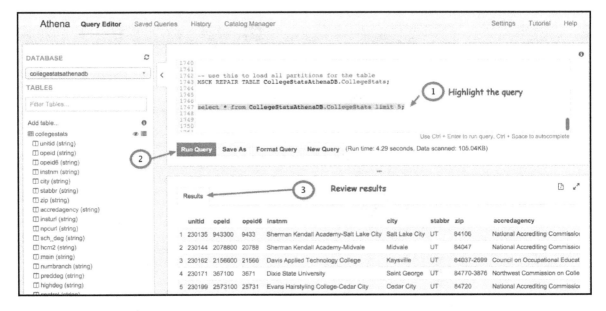

Figure 2.29: Athena preview data

This completes the creation of a table in an Athena database. Next, we will see how to visualize this data in QuickSight.

Creating a new QuickSight dataset from Athena

Now that data is accessible via Athena, follow these steps to create a new dataset in QuickSight:

1. From the QuickSight home page, click on **Manage data**.
2. Select **New data set** and then select **Athena**.
3. For the **Data source name**, enter the same name as the Athena database; `CollegeStatsAthenaDB`.

4. Click on **Validate connection** to confirm that QuickSight can connect to Athena. After it is validated, click on **Create data source** to complete the data source creation, as shown in the following screenshot:

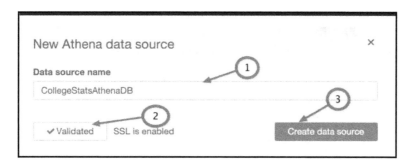

Figure 2.30: Athena data source

5. Select the table `collegestats` from the table selection and then select **Edit/Preview data**, as shown in the following screenshot:

Figure 2.31: Athena table selection

6. The table has over 1700 fields; for this demonstration, we will focus only on enrollment-related fields and only for public colleges. For this, we will use the QuickSight option to report data based on custom SQL, as shown in the following screenshot:

Figure 2.32: Athena data source import to SPICE

The query is as follows:

```
select Year, UNITID, INSTNM, CITY, STABBR, ZIP,region,
ADM_RATE,
CASE WHEN (SATVRMID='NULL') THEN '0' ELSE SATVRMID END as
    SAT_Midpoint_Reading,
CASE WHEN (SATMTMID='NULL') THEN '0' ELSE SATMTMID END as
    SAT_Midpoint_Math,
CASE WHEN (SATWRMID='NULL') THEN '0' ELSE SATWRMID END as
SAT_Midpoint_Writing,
CASE WHEN (SAT_AVG='NULL') THEN '0' ELSE SAT_AVG END as
    SAT_Average,
CASE WHEN (ACTCMMID='NULL') THEN '0' ELSE ACTCMMID END as
    ACT_Midpoint_Cumulative,
CASE WHEN (ACTENMID='NULL') THEN '0' ELSE ACTENMID END as
    ACT_Midpoint_English,
CASE WHEN (ACTMTMID='NULL') THEN '0' ELSE ACTMTMID END as
```

```
    ACT_Midpoint_Math,
CASE WHEN (ACTWRMID='NULL') THEN '0' ELSE ACTWRMID END as
    ACT_Midpoint_Writing
CASE WHEN (NPT4_PUB='NULL') THEN '0' ELSE NPT4_PUB END as
    Average_Net_Tuition_Price,
CASE WHEN (UGDS='NULL') THEN '0' ELSE UGDS END as
    Enrollment_All_Count,
CASE WHEN (TUITIONFEE_IN='NULL') THEN '0' ELSE TUITIONFEE_IN
    END as Average_InState_Tuition,
CASE WHEN (TUITIONFEE_OUT='NULL') THEN '0' ELSE TUITIONFEE_OUT
    END as Average_OutState_Tuition
from CollegeStatsAthenaDB.CollegeStats
where main = '1'
and HIGHDEG = '4'
and CONTROL = '1';
```

7. Update the data type of all numeric fields to integer as this will help the reporting and visualization.

8. Click on **Save & visualize** to analyze this data.

9. Change the visualization type to vertical stacked bar chart; set the **Enrollment_All_Count** to a **measure**; select **X axis** as **Year**, **Value** as **Enrollement_All_Count**, and **Group/Color** as **STABBAR**. Finally, to focus only on top states by count, filter the chart with **Enrollment_All_Count** greater than 200,000.

10. This will give you a pretty useful trend that shows that the state of Ohio has a drop of enrollment from **219K** in year **2010** to **217K** in year **2013** in comparison to the state of Texas where enrollment grew from **438K** to **467K** for the same time period, as shown in the following screenshot:

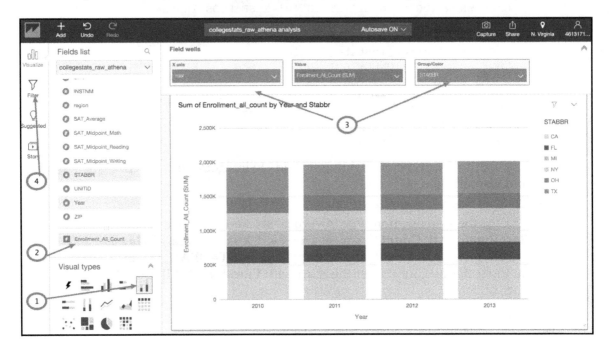

Figure 2.33: Athena bar chart

This completes the loading of data from Athena to QuickSight.

Loading data from Salesforce to QuickSight

In this section, we will review how QuickSight can connect to your Salesforce account and visualize data.

Pre-requisites

You must have valid Salesforce credentials and objects or reports that you have access to in Salesforce. QuickSight supports the enterprise edition, unlimited edition, and developer edition of Salesforce.

 Currently Salesforce joined reports are not supported by QuickSight.

Creating a dataset from Salesforce

In this section, we will review how to connect to your Salesforce account and report customer accounts. Follow these steps:

1. From the QuickSight home page, click on **Manage data**.
2. Next, select **New data set** and then select **Salesforce** option.
3. Type a name for this data source as `SalesforceCustomers` and click on the **Create data source** button, as shown in the following screenshot:

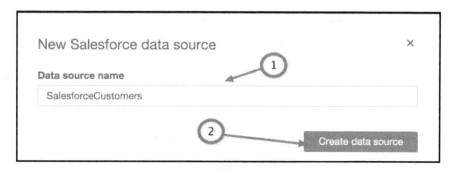

Figure 2.34: Salesforce new source

4. You will be redirected to the Salesforce login page, enter your username and password.

5. Now that QuickSight is connected to your Salesforce account, you can choose the data element from Salesforce. The data element can either be a report or an object; for this demonstration, select **OBJECT** and further select **ContactCleanInfo** and then click on the **Select** button, as shown in the following screenshot:

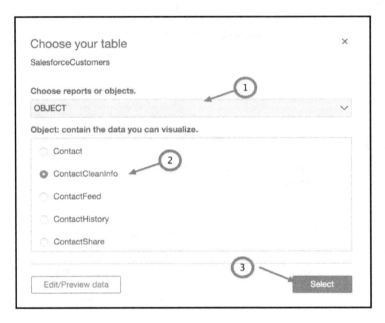

Figure 2.35: Salesforce contact object selection

6. You will get confirmation that data has been successfully loaded to SPICE, as shown in the next screenshot. From here, click on **Visualize** to start a new analysis in QuickSight.

Figure 2.36: Salesforce dataset creation confirmation

7. Now, in QuickSight analysis editor, change the visualization type to tree map, select **AccountId** field for **Size** and **MailingCity** field for **Group by**. This visualization now shows that the top city with accounts is **TAMPA**, followed by **SAN JOSE**, as shown in the following screenshot:

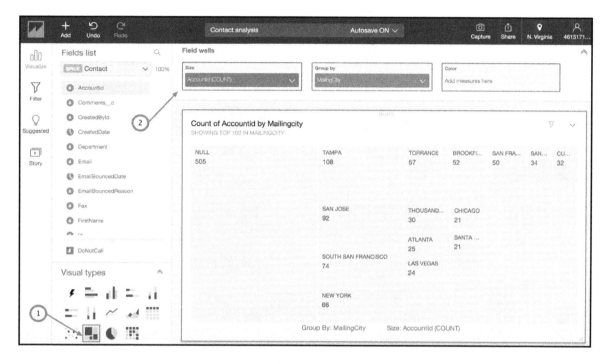

Figure 2.37: Salesforce chart

This completes the Salesforce data set creation in QuickSight.

Editing existing datasets

In this section, we will review how QuickSight allows us to edit existing datasets. Follow these steps to edit an existing dataset:

1. From the QuickSight home page, click on **Manage data**.
2. Under **Your Data Sets**, select the specific dataset you want to edit.
3. For this demonstration, let's select the S3 data set named USACensus-S3-DataSet, as shown in the following screenshot:

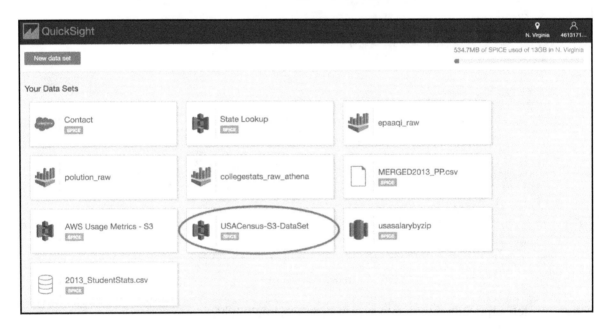

Figure 2.38 Select existing dataset

4. You will next see options to **Delete data set** or **Edit data set**, as shown in the following screenshot:

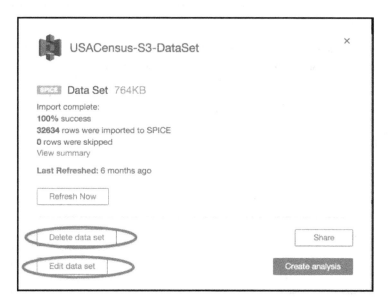

Figure 2.39: Edit or delete S3 dataset

5. If you select **Delete data set**, you will get a warning regarding related analyses that will be impacted. The analysis will not be deleted, but the next time you use such an analysis, you will be prompted to select a new data set to enable visualizations. Click on **Delete** if you really wish to delete or **Cancel** to skip the delete.

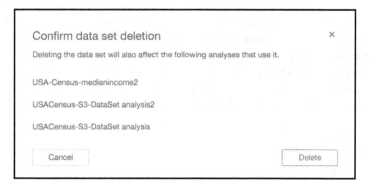

Figure 2.40: Delete data set confirmation

6. If you want to edit, click on **Edit data set**, which will take you to a new page where you can change data types, add new columns, and change data types as shown in the following screenshot. We will discuss this further in Chapter 3, *SPICE up Your Data*.

Figure 2.41: Edit data set

This concludes the *editing existing datasets* section.

Summary

Amazon has a robust big data ecosystem component that covers data collection, storage, analysis, and orchestration to support the end-to-end needs for business intelligence. The QuickSight service is part of the analysis component and it has built connectors to onboard data from the various sources including S3, RDS, Redshift, Athena, and Salesforce and this list is continuing to grow. AWS Data Pipeline makes end-to-end orchestration easier and reduces development efforts. In the next chapter, we will look deeper into SPICE, which makes QuickSight responsive even on large datasets.

3
SPICE up Your Data

SPICE is the accelerator of QuickSight, delivering interactive visualizations on large datasets at lightning speed. SPICE is engineered with parallelism, automatic replications, and a rich calculation engine to serve thousands of users, who can simultaneously perform fast interactive queries.

In this chapter, we will take an in-depth look at this component via the following topics:

- SPICE – overview and architecture
- Importing data to SPICE
- Joining datasets
- Enriching data using functions
- Filtering your datasets

SPICE – overview and architecture

SPICE is an abbreviation for Super-fast, Parallel, In-memory, Calculation, Engine and is the brain of QuickSight. It can source data from S3, RDS databases, Redshift, RDBMS databases, and, in future, EMR, Kinesis, and DynamoDB. SPICE has a great toolset of functions that can do lightweight transformation of data in memory, thereby eliminating the need for traditional **ETL (Extract Transform and Load)**.

The following diagram shows the position of SPICE in an overall BI solution. On the left-hand side you see the various sources that can push data to SPICE. Data from them is cached by SPICE, which uses a combination of columnar storage, in-memory technologies, machine code generation, data compression, and auto-replication for high availability. The results from SPICE serve QuickSight analysis and, in future, SPICE will integrate with AWS BI partners such as Tableau, TIBCO, Qlick, and Domo using its SQL-like interface.

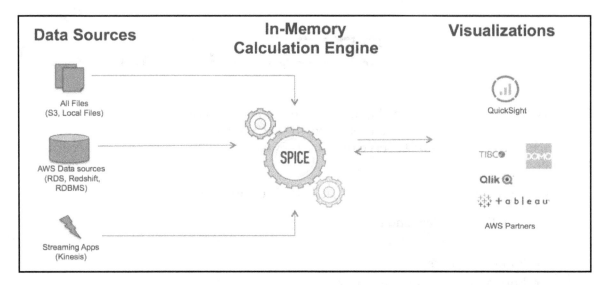

Figure 3.1: SPICE architecture

For each paid QuickSight user, you will get 10 GB of SPICE capacity. This SPICE capacity is pooled across users of the Amazon QuickSight account; therefore, the more users you add, the bigger will be the shared pool. Each QuickSight account also gets 1 GB free capacity. In the next few sections, we will review how to enrich and filter datasets using SPICE.

Importing data into SPICE

This was seen in Chapter 2, *Exploring Any Data*, where we imported data to SPICE. When you import data, you will see the spinning icon; once the spinning is completed, you get a summary of the number of rows imported.

If any rows were skipped, you can view them by clicking on **View import summary...** , as shown in the following screenshot:

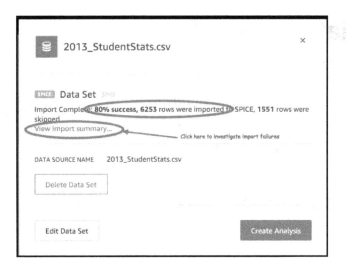

Figure 3.2: Importing data into SPICE

When you click on **View import summary…**, you will get more details about the failures, specifically the fields and the reason, as shown in the following screenshot. You can further click on **Edit data set** and fix the issues.

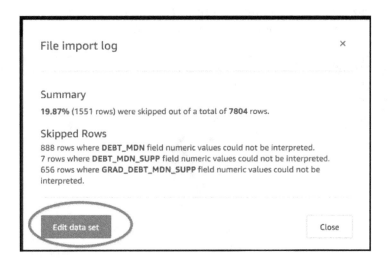

Figure 3.3: Summary after import

This completes the section on importing datasets to SPICE; next, we will review how to join datasets.

Joining data in SPICE

Joining tables is a very common requirement for data analysis and SPICE makes this effort a breeze. To understand this feature, let's go for a real use case. In the Chapter 2, *Exploring Any Data, Loading data from Redshift to Quicksight* section, we had uploaded USACensusSalarybyZip.csv, which has salary and population information by USA zip code. Now let's upload another file that has mapping of zip codes to USA states and cities and then we will join this with the other dataset in SPICE.

Loading data to Redshift

First we need to load this new file to Redshift as a table. Here are the steps to load the data to Redshift:

1. Download the data file from this GitHub location: https://github.com/rnadipa lli/quicksight/blob/master/sampledata/USAZipCodes.csv.

2. Upload the file to your S3 bucket.

3. Create a new AWS data pipeline to upload S3 data to your Redshift cluster and call it USAZIPCODES. You can clone the data pipeline created in the Chapter 2, *Exploring Any Data, Creating and executing an AWS Data Pipeline* section. The following is a screenshot of the new data pipeline:

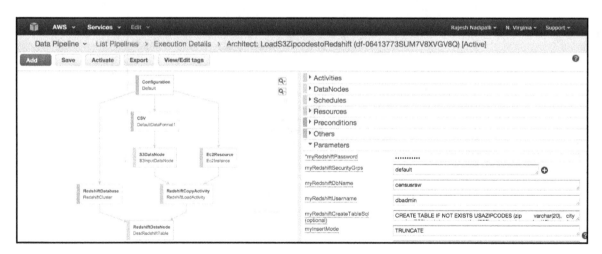

Figure 3.4: AWS pipeline zip code

4. For your reference, I have uploaded this data pipeline at `https://github.com/rnadipalli/quicksight/blob/master/awsdatapipelines/LoadS3ZipcodetoRedshiftpipeline.json`.

5. Once this data is uploaded to Redshift, you can use a database management tool like SQL Workbench/J to view and query the data.

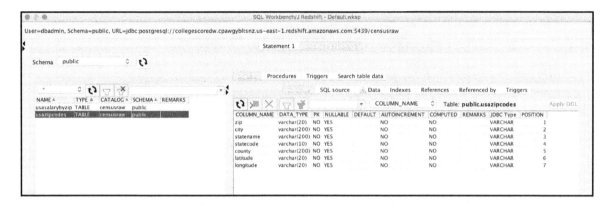

Figure 3.5: USA zip codes table description

 You can download the SQL Workbench/J software from `http://www.sql-workbench.net/downloads.html`.

This completes the loading of new data to Redshift; next, we will review the steps to join the two tables and create a new dataset.

Creating a new joined dataset

Now that we have two tables in the Redshift instance, we follow these steps to create a new dataset and load it to SPICE:

1. From the QuickSight home page, click on **Manage data**.
2. Click on **New data set** and then select the **Redshift** option.

3. Next, enter the details of the Redshift data source and select the new table that was created, as shown in the following screenshot:

Figure 3.6: Preparing data after loading to Redshift

4. Now, in the data preparation page, select both the `usasalarybyzip` and `usazipcodes` tables as shown in the next figure.

5. Next, click on the **?** sign between the two tables to configure the join criteria. You have the following options for join criteria:
   - **Inner**: This gives only records that have matching values in the join columns from the two tables. This is the most commonly used and default option and is also shown in the next screenshot, where the join field is zip code.
   - **Left**: This performs a left outer join, returning all records from the left-hand side table and only records that have a value in the join column for the right-hand side table.
   - **Right**: This performs a right outer join, returning all records from the right-hand side table and only records that have a value in the join column for the left-hand side table.
   - **Outer**: This performs a full outer join and returns records from both tables regardless of the values in the join columns.

6. Click on **Apply** to activate the join and see the results:

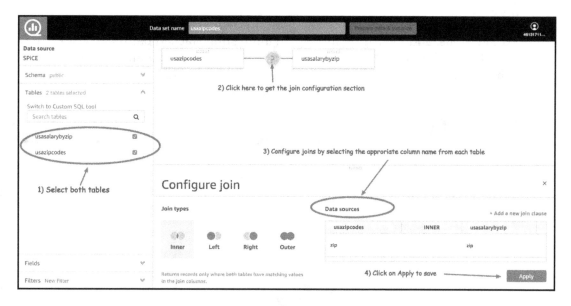

Figure 3.7: Join using SPICE

7. SPICE then shows the resultant combined dataset, as shown in the following screenshot. Next, click on **Prepare data & visualize** to visualize the joined dataset.

Figure 3.8: Prepare and visualize the joined dataset

8. Now, in QuickSight visualization, you can change the visualization type, dimensions, and measures and see an interesting stacked bar that shows which city has the best average salary in orange bars; the corresponding population is shown in blue bars. The following screenshot shows that **Pound Ridge** has an average salary of $219,554 and a population of 4,764:

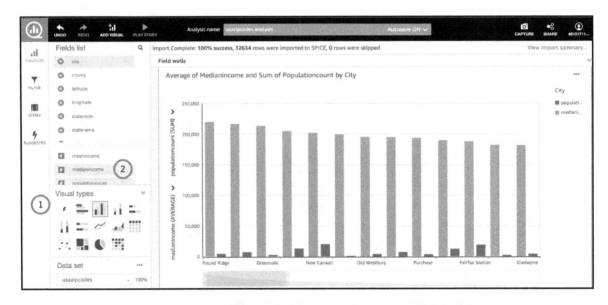

Figure 3.9: Visualization on joined data

This completes the joining dataset section; next, let's review other ways to enrich data in SPICE.

Enriching your data

One of the exciting features of SPICE is the ability to transform data and also create additional derived fields. Let's look at this feature with an example; follow these steps to add a new derived field to the dataset we just created:

1. From the QuickSight home page, click on **Manage data**.
2. Select the **usasalarybyzipandcity** that was created in the previous *Joining data in SPICE* section and then click on **Edit data set**.
3. Select **New Field** and then follow the wizard on the right to create a new derived field.

4. In this example, we are going to use the `toUppper` function in the formula and convert the statement name to uppercase.

Figure 3.10: Derived column

This completes the example on how to create a new derived field. Now let's review the various functions available in SPICE.

Arithmetic and comparison operators

For numeric data types, SPICE allows the following arithmetic and comparison operators in calculated fields:

- Addition (+)

- Subtraction (-)

- Multiplication (*)

- Division (/)

- Equal (=)

- Not equal (!=)

- Greater than (>)

- Greater than or equal (>=)

- Less than (<)

- Less than or equal (<=)

- AND

- OR

Let's take up an example: we need a new column that has the difference between mean and median. The formula for this calculated column is shown in the screenshot here:

Figure 3.11: Arithmetic functions

In the next section, we will review conditional functions supported in SPICE.

Conditional functions

SPICE has the following conditional functions, which are very useful in several situations:

- `ifelse`

- `coalesce`

- `isNotNull`

- `isNull`

- `nullIf`

Let's review each function in detail.

ifelse

The `ifelse` function conditionally executes a group of statements depending on the value of an expression. Let's take an example of calculating an income score based on the range of median income for the data of various zip codes:

- If income is less than 30,000, set the score to 1

- If income is between 30,000 and 50,000, then the score is 2

- Else if income is greater than 50,000, then the score is 3

The formula for this expression is shown in the following screenshot:

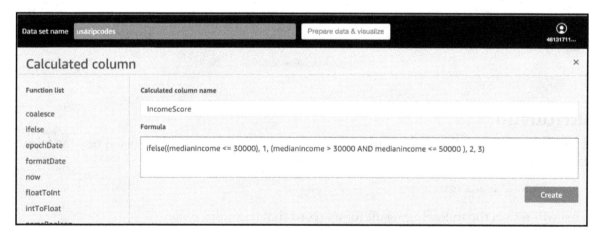

Figure 3.12: ifelse function

coalesce

The coalesce function returns the value of the first argument that is not null. When a non-null value is found, the remaining arguments in the list are not evaluated. This is very useful when you need to substitute the column with the best available options in case the data has null values.

Let's see an example of how this can be used in our zip code salary dataset, which has some nulls for county. In such cases, let's substitute with what is available, such as city name. Here is a screenshot showing how to create a formula for such a requirement:

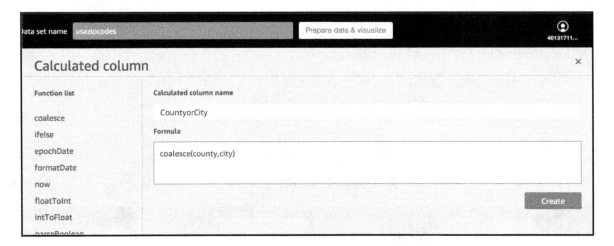

Figure 3.13: coalesce function

isNotNull

The isNotNull function returns true if the expression is not null; otherwise it returns false. Let's see an example of how to use this function:

```
isNotNull(medianincome)
```

This will return the following result for a record that has valid data:

```
true
```

isNull

The `isNull` function returns true if the expression is null; otherwise, it returns false. Let's see an example of this:

```
isNull(medianincome)
```

It will return the following result for a record that has valid data:

```
false
```

nullIf

The `nullIf` function compares two expressions. If the two expressions match, it will return null; otherwise, it will return the first expression. Let's see an example of how to use this function:

```
nullIf ({address}, 'NA')
```

Suppose the field has the following values:

```
644 TenTen Road, Apex, NC
NA
567 Church Street, Raleigh NC
```

With the `nullIf` function, you will get the following results:

```
644 TenTen Road, Apex, NC
null
567 Church Street, Raleigh NC
```

This completes the conditional functions section; next, we will review date functions in SPICE.

Date functions

SPICE has the following functions for date data types:

- `epochDate`

- `formatDate`

- `now`

- `dateDiff`

- `extract`

- `truncDate`

Let's review them in detail.

epochDate

Often, we get data that has an epoch string, which represents a date and time in numeric format. SPICE has a function to make this conversion automatic and it is called `epochDate`. Let's see an example of how to use this function:

```
epochDate(1469995419)
```

This will return the following result:

```
2016-07-31T20:03:38.000Z
```

formatDate

In several scenarios, you will need to change the format of the date field to suit your reporting needs as per your enterprise needs; for this, SPICE has the `formatDate` function.

Let's see an example usage of this function:

```
formatDate('31/7/16 15:30:27', 'dd MM yyyy', 'America/Los_Angeles')
```

This will result in the following:

```
31 Jul 2016
```

Here are some additional notes on the usage of this function:

- The date can be provided from a `date` field or an `integer` field containing an epoch date

- The format syntax used is as per the Joda project definition (http://www.joda.org/joda-time/apidocs/org/joda/time/format/DateTimeFormat.html)

- The last parameter is timezone which, if not passed, is defaulted to UTC

now

In several scenarios, you will need to know the current date and time when the report is run and use it for further calculations, for example, showing the metrics for the current quarter based on today's date. For such scenarios, the `now` function can be used and it returns the date in the UTC time zone as follows:

```
2016-07-31T19:20:03:003Z
```

dateDiff

The `dateDiff` function operates on two date fields and returns the difference in days between them. Let's see an example usage of this function:

```
dateDiff('7/10/16', '7/13/16')
```

It will result in the following:

```
3
```

extract and truncDate

The `extract` and `truncDate` functions are quite similar and accept two parameters, where the first parameter is the period and second parameter is a date field. The `extract` function returns a portion of the date value in integer format and `truncDate` returns a date truncated to the period.

The following are the valid periods you can request:

- YYYY: Returns the year portion of the date
- MM: Returns the month portion of the date
- DD: Returns the day portion of the date
- WD: Returns the day of the week as an integer, with Sunday being 0
- HH: Returns the hour portion of the date
- MI: Returns the minute portion of the date
- SS: Returns the second portion of the date

Let's see an example usage of this function for a date field, `LineItemStartTime`, to get just the year portion of the date:

```
truncDate('YYYY',LineItemStartTime)
extract('YYYY',LineItemStartTime)
```

For a date string `2016-08-06T00:00:00.000Z`, `truncDate` will return `2016-01-01T00:00:00.000Z` and extract will return `2016`. This is also shown in the screenshot here:

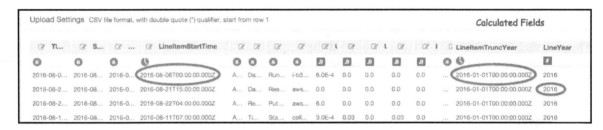

Figure 3.14: Extract and truncDate

This completes the date functions; next, let's review numeric functions.

Numeric functions

SPICE provides the following numeric functions:

- `ceil`

- `decimalToInt`

- `floor`

- `intToDecimal`

- `round`

Let's review these functions in detail.

ceil

This function rounds a decimal value to the next highest integer. Let's see an example usage of it:

```
ceil(20.14)
```

It will return:

```
21
```

decimalToInt

This function converts a decimal value to an integer by stripping the decimal portion of the number. It does not do any rounding. Let's see an example usage of this function:

```
decimalToInt(20.14)
```

It will return:

```
20
```

floor

This function rounds a decimal value to the next lowest integer. Let's see an example usage of this function:

```
floor(21.80)
```

It will return:

```
21
```

intToDecimal

This function converts an integer value to decimal data type. Let's see an example usage of it:

```
intToDecimal(20)
```

It will return this:

```
20.0
```

round

This function will round a decimal value to the closest integer or closest decimal to the scale specified. This is useful when you are dealing with currency and want to have all data with two decimal places.

Let's see an example usage of this function:

```
round(54.1482,2)
```

It returns:

```
54.15
```

This completes numeric functions; next, let's review string functions.

String functions

SPICE supports the following functions on string data types:

- concat

- left

- locate

- ltrim

- parseDate

- parseDecimal

- parseInt

- replace

- right

- rtrim

- strlen

- substring

- toLower

- toString

- toUpper

- trim

Let's review the string functions in detail.

concat

This function takes two or more expressions and concatenates them as one string. Let's see an example usage of this function:

```
concat('Mr ','John ','Smith')
```

It will return the following as one string:

```
Mr John Smith
```

left

This function returns the leftmost portion of the string based on the number of characters you specify. It takes two parameters; the first is an expression and the second is the number of characters. Let's see an example usage of this function:

```
left('2900 S Salem Street',6)
```

It returns:

```
2900 S
```

locate

This function locates the position of a substring within another string. You can optionally provide which occurrence you want to select in case it has multiple occurrences. Let's see an example usage of this function:

```
locate('apple or orange or banana',2)
```

It will return the following:

```
17
```

ltrim

This function removes leading whitespace characters and is pretty useful if you are receiving data from a source that does not have good data quality. Let's see an example usage of this function:

```
ltrim('  John Smith')
```

It returns the following:

```
John Smith
```

parseDate

This function parses a string to determine if it contains a valid date in the specified format and returns a standard date format: `yyyy-MM-ddTkk:mm:ss.SSSZ`. It will skip if the input string does not match the format.

 The `parseDate` function is not supported for use with SPICE datasets. It supports file, RDS, and Redshift datasets.

Let's see an example usage of this function:

```
parseDate('12-31-2016','MM-dd-yyyy')
```

It will return:

```
12-31-2016T00:00:00.000Z
```

However, `parseDate('07/31/2016','MM-dd-yyyy')`, will skip this record.

parseDecimal

This function parses a string to determine if it contains a decimal value. The function returns a decimal data type if there is valid data; if not, it will skip that data.

Let's see an example usage of this function:

```
parseDecimal('46')
```

It will return

```
46.0
```

However, `parseDecimal('4.35')` will return `4.35` and `parseDecimal('2a')` will skip this record.

parseInt

This function parses a string to determine whether it contains an integer value. The function returns an integer if there is a valid integer. If the string has a decimal, the data is rounded to the nearest integer; if the string has no numeric data, then that record will be skipped.

Let's see an example usage of this function:

```
parseInt('46')
```

It will return

```
46
```

However, `parseInt('4.35')` will return `4` and `parseInt('2a')` will skip this record.

replace

This function replaces a part of a string with another string as specified. The function is useful when there is a global replacement required to the data without updating it. Let's see an example usage of this function. You have state codes and want to replace them with complete state names, where the state code field is called `STABBR`. The new field expression will be as follows:

```
replace(replace(replace(STABBR,'UT','Utah'),'VT','Vermont'),'VA','Virgi
nia')
```

The following figure shows the original field and the new calculated field:

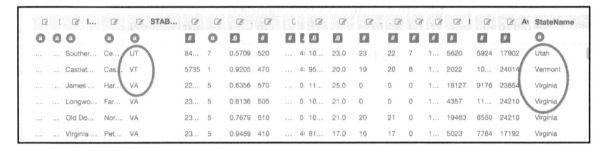

Figure 3.15: replace function

right

This function returns the rightmost portion of the string based on the number of characters you specify. It takes two parameters: the first is an expression and the second is the number of characters. Let's see an example usage of this function:

```
right('2900 S Salem Street',6)
```

It will return the following:

```
Street
```

rtrim

This function removes trailing whitespace characters and is pretty useful if you are receiving data from a source that does not have good data quality. Let's see an example usage:

```
rtrim('John Smith    ')
```

This returns the following:

```
John Smith
```

strlen

This function returns the number of characters in the string, including whitespaces. Let's see an example usage of this function:

```
strlen('John Smith')
```

It returns the following:

```
10
```

substring

This function returns a portion of the expression by using three parameters, the first being the expression, the next being the starting location, and last being the length. Let's see an example usage:

```
substring('apple or orange or banana',6,9)
```

This will return the following:

```
or orange
```

toLower

This function formats the string to lowercase. Let's see an example usage of this function:

```
toLower('Baskin Ridge, NJ')
```

The result is:

```
baskin ridge, nj
```

toString

This function formats the input expression as a string data type.

Let's see an example usage:

```
toString('44.59')
```

It will return

```
44.59
```

toUpper

This function formats the string to uppercase. Let's see an example usage of this function:

```
toUpper('Baskin Ridge, NJ')
```

It will return:

```
BASKIN RIDGE, NJ
```

trim

This function removes leading and trailing whitespace characters:

```
ltrim('  John Smith    ')
```

It will return the following:

```
John Smith
```

This completes a review of all functions and the enrichment section in SPICE. In the next section, we will see how to filter data using SPICE.

Filtering data using SPICE

With SPICE, we can refine data in a dataset. Each filter applies to only one field, which can be a regular or a derived field. We can apply multiple filters to the same field or different fields. Let's review this functionality in detail.

Adding new filters

Let's see how to use the filtering features on the zip code salary data. We will filter the dataset for records that have median income between $30,000 and $60,000 and for states in the north east (NH, MA, NY, CT, and NJ).

We will achieve this in two key steps: filter on the numeric `medianincome` and then filter on the text field `statecode`.

Filter on medianincome

Follow these steps to add a filter on the numeric field `medianincome`:

1. On the data preparation page, click on the **Filters** pane.
2. Next click on **New filter**.
3. Next select `medianincome` as shown in the following screenshot:

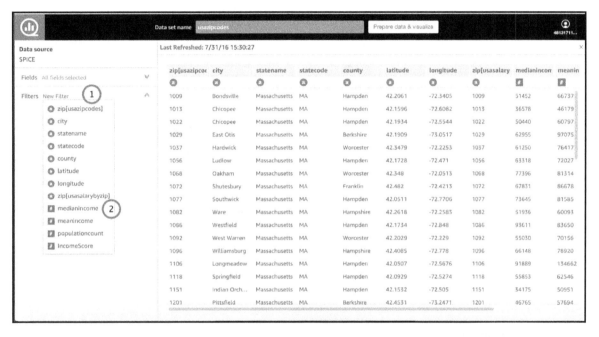

Figure 3.16: Filter on medianincome

4. Click on the text **Equals – none**, which will then expand the various filter options, as shown in the next screenshot.
5. Select the filter criteria as **Between** and the range from 30,000 to 60,000.

6. Next click on **Apply** and this will save this filter for the `medianincome` field.

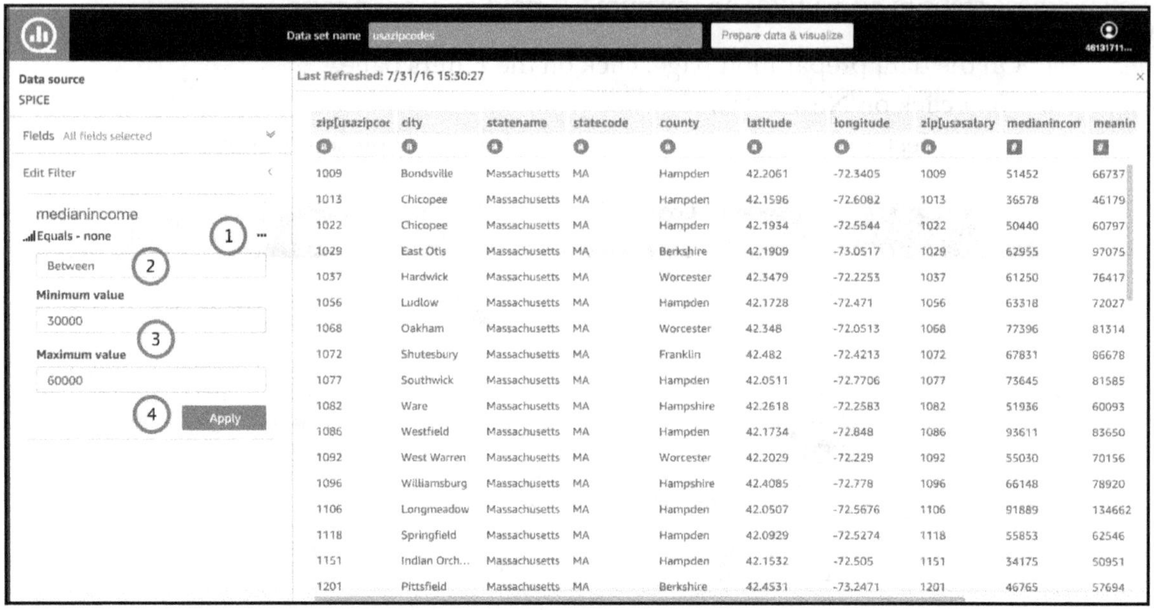

Figure 3.17: Medianincome range

This completes the filter on `medianincome` which is a numeric field; next, let's review how to filter on the `statecode`, which is a string.

Filter on statecode

Follow these steps to add a filter on the `statecode` text field:

1. On the data preparation page, click on the **Filters** pane.
2. Next, click on **New filter**.

3. Select the `statecode` field, as shown in the following screenshot:

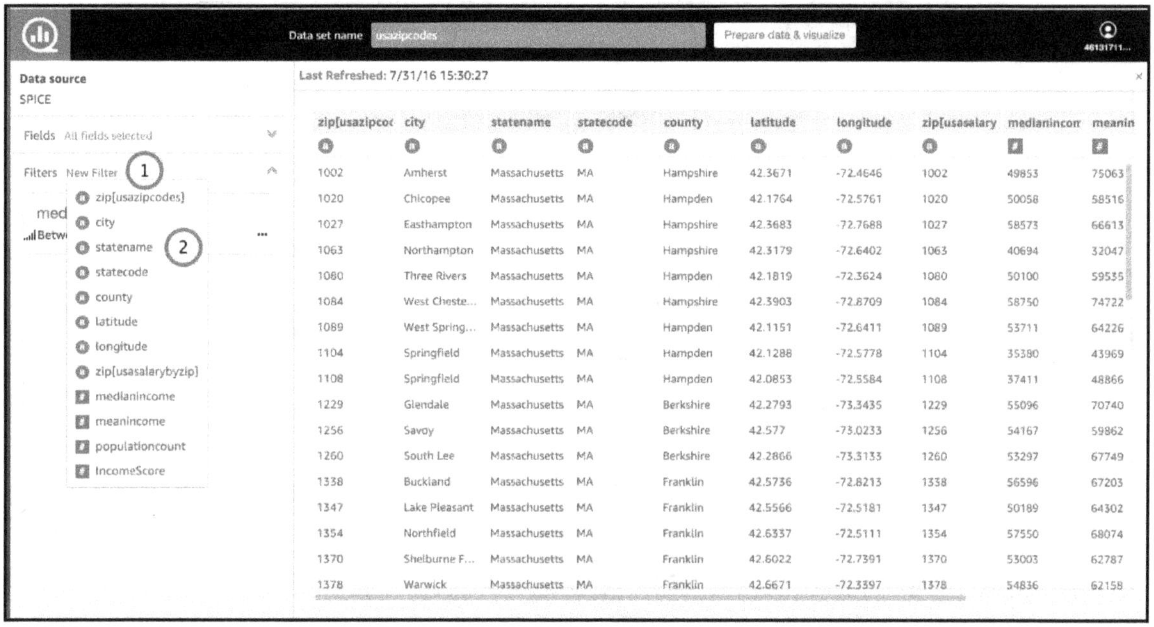

Figure 3.18: Filter statecode

4. Click on **Include – all** to expand the various filter options, as shown in the next screenshot.
5. Select the filter criteria as **Custom filter list**.
6. Add the five northeastern states (NH, MA, NY, CT, and NJ) one at a time using the + sign.

7. After this, click on **Apply** to activate this filter.

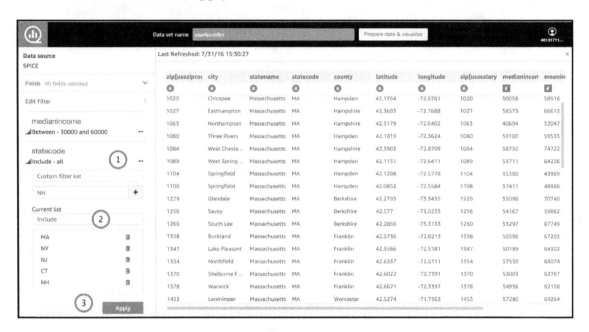

Figure 3.19: statecode list

With these steps, we have now successfully filtered the dataset to median income between 30,000 and 60,000 and for the selected northeastern states. In the next section, we will review how to edit existing filters.

Editing existing filters

We can edit existing filter criteria and enable or disable them. Let's review this feature in detail.

Changing existing filter criteria

Let's edit the `statecode` filter and add the state of Maine (ME) to the filter. Use the following steps to achieve this goal:

1. On the data preparation page, click on the **Filters** pane.
2. Click on **Include – NH and more**.

3. Add the statecode ME to the list.
4. Click on **Apply** as shown in the following screenshot:

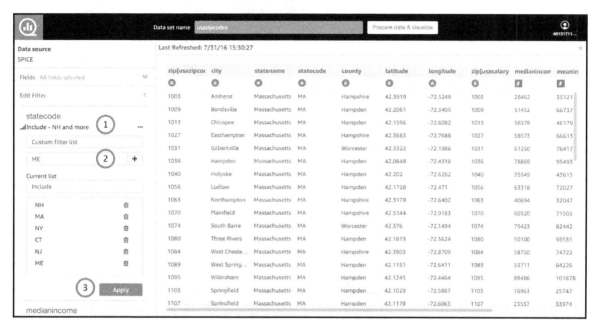

Figure 3.20: statecode filter edit

This completes the section on editing existing filters. Next, we will review how to disable and delete existing filters.

Enable, disable, or delete a filter

We can also disable an existing filter using the data preparation page. This could be handy in case you want to temporarily disable a filter and then later enable it. Here are the steps to disable or enable an existing filter:

1. On the data preparation page, click on the **Filters** pane.
2. Decide on the filter you want to enable/disable. For this example, let's consider the statecode filter added in the earlier steps.
3. Click on the three **...** next to the filter name as shown in the following screenshot.

4. Next click on **Disable filter**, **Enable filter**, or **Delete filter** as desired.

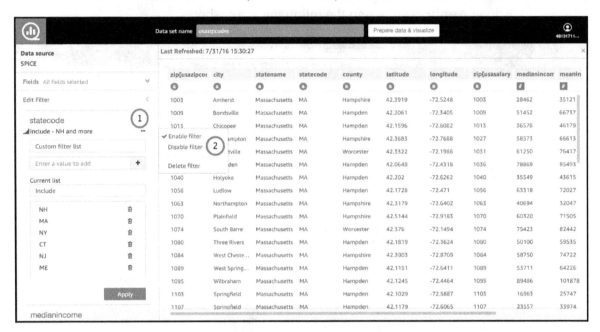

Figure 3.21: Enable or disable filter

Summary

SPICE is the brain of QuickSight and enables it to scale to thousands of users who can all simultaneously perform fast interactive analyses from a variety of AWS data sources. After data is imported to SPICE, it can be joined with other datasets and also enriched with a wide range of string, date, and numeric functions. Additionally, we can filter data based to restrict what dataset gets analyzed. The capacity of SPICE is 10 GB per user and is pooled across all users in the account that also allows organizations to automatically increase capacity as they grow the team size.

In the next chapter, we will see how to create a variety of interactive and effective visuals on top of the SPICE engine, empowering data analysts and management to make data-driven decisions.

4

Intuitive Visualizations

QuickSight can create a wide variety of visuals on different datasets imported to SPICE. In this chapter, we will look at visualization capabilities in detail. The following topics will be covered:

- Creating an analysis
- Creating various charts and tables
- Recommendations on selecting the right visualizations
- Telling a story
- Sharing dashboards

From data to visualization using QuickSight

Let's review the steps involved in getting to the visualization stage from source data.

1. First, to work with data, we need to create QuickSight datasets, which typically include one or more tables, or files, from the source.
2. Optionally, if the dataset needs some cleanup or format changes, you can prepare data using the QuickSight SPICE engine.
3. From each dataset, we can create one or more analyses, which are containers for visualizations.
4. Within each analysis, we can create one or more visualizations. A visualization is a graphical representation on a dataset enabling consumers to get insights from the data.
5. Optionally, you can add scenes to the default story to provide a narrative about the insights.

6. Optionally, you can create read-only snapshots of the visualizations as dashboards and share the insights with others.

 For further information on dataset creation, refer to `Chapter 3`, *Spice up Your Data.*

The preceding steps to get to visualizations are depicted in the following diagram:

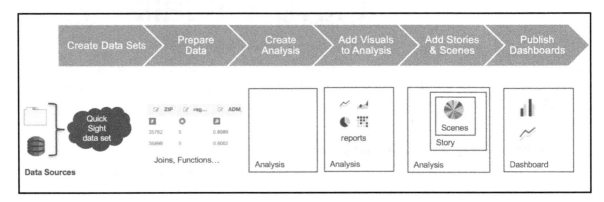

Figure 4.1: From source data to visualizations

Building analyses from datasets

An analysis is the foundation for visualizing your datasets. It is a container for a set of related visuals. Each analysis also contains a default story, which can be used to step through different iterations of an analysis over time; for example, you may want to share the same visual but with different filters like year/region and see them in a sequence as scenes.

An analysis is generally based on one dataset but QuickSight allows you to join datasets under one analysis, although a given visual can only have data from one dataset. You can have a maximum of 20 visuals in an analysis.

Let's look into the detailed steps for creating a new dataset and then an analysis on top of that dataset.

Creating a new dataset

Before we can create an analysis, we need a dataset. Let's review the steps to create a new dataset:

1. For this example, we will create a new dataset based on a USA census data file that we have in S3 storage called `USACensusSalarybyZip.csv`. Click first on **Manage data** and then on **New data set** as shown in the following screenshot:

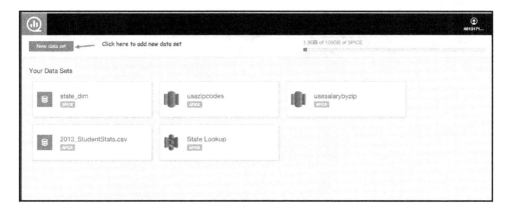

Figure 4.2: Creating a new dataset

The S3 data file `USACensusSalarybyZip.csv` is at the following GitHub location: `https://github.com/rnadipalli/quicksight/blob/master/sampledata/USACensusSalarybyZip.csv`.

2. Enter the **Data source name**, upload the S3 manifest file and then click **Connect** as shown in the following screenshot:

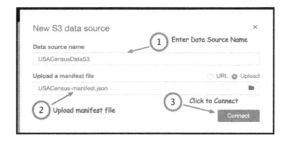

Figure 4.3: Uploading S3 data

For your reference, the manifest file for the S3 data file is in the following GitHub location: `https://github.com/rnadipalli/quicksight/blob/master/sampledata/USACensus-manifest.json`.

3. Now the source data is imported to a dataset in QuickSight. This is shown in the next screenshot. In this page, provide a name for the dataset; add column headers by double-clicking in the gray column headers and finally save. This will create a new dataset with the name, `USACensus-S3-DataSet`.

Figure 4.4: Save dataset

This completes the creation of the dataset of `USACensus-S3-DataSet` which will appear as one of your datasets under **Manage data**.

Creating a new analysis

Now that we have the dataset, let's build a new analysis using that dataset, which will act as the container for visuals. Here are the steps to create a new analysis:

1. From the QuickSight home page, click on **New analysis**. This will show the list of existing datasets. Select the newly created dataset `USACensus-S3-DataSet` as

shown in the following screenshot:

Figure 4.5: Create analysis – use existing dataset

2. After you select your dataset, you will see a pop-up as shown in the following screenshot; click on **Create Analysis** to use that dataset for your analysis.

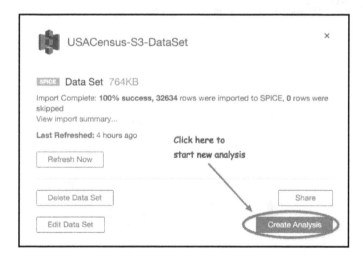

Figure 4.6: Create analysis pop-up

3. You will see the analysis page show up where you can change the analysis name (optional) in the application bar.

This completes the creation of a new data analysis with the name `USACensus-S3-DataSet analysis`. Next, we will add a visual to the analysis.

Adding a visual to an analysis

Now that we have an analysis (container), we can add visuals to the analysis using the following steps:

1. In the application bar, click on **Add Visual**.
2. Next, in the **Fields list**, configure your dimensions and measures. Dimensions are typically lists of values like products. Customers and measures are metrics like customer score and product quality. In our example, set the `ZipCode` as dimension and leave the `MeanIncome`, `MedianIncome` and `PopulationCount` as measure. To change a field to a measure, click on the **v** icon next to the field of interest.
3. Choose the appropriate visual. For our example, let's select bar chart; see the following screenshot:

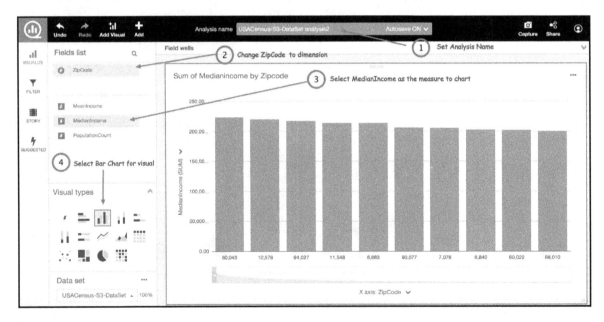

Figure 4.7: Select visualization type, dimension, and measures

If you don't know which visual will work for the data, select the **Suggested** option and QuickSight will select the best options.

4. In our example, the *Y* axis median income should be average and this can be changed by clicking on the **>** sign next to the **MedianIncome(SUM)** text as shown in the following screenshot:

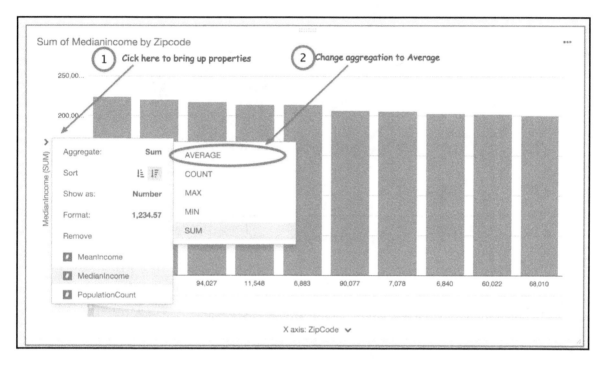

Figure 4.8: Change Y axis aggregation type

5. Let's do advance formatting to the `MedianIncome` field by first selecting the field, and then click on **More formatting options** as shown in the following screenshot:

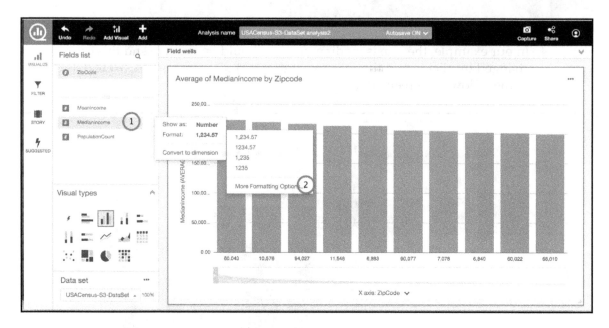

Figure 4. 9: Median income formatting

6. Next from the **Format** pane on the left, select the **Data Type** as **Currency**, **Decimal places** as 0 and **Units** as **Thousands**. This will make the *Y* axis easy to read.

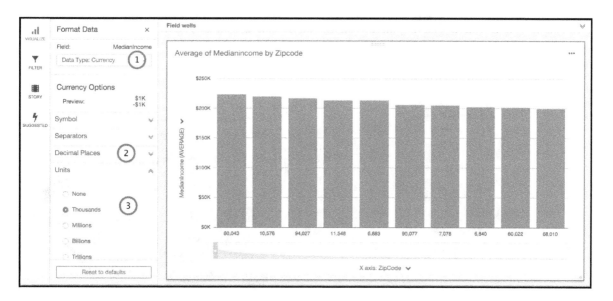

Figure 4.10: Median income advanced formatting options

7. Next, for the finishing touch, change the `ZipCode` formatting to a standard number with no comma separator. Now the chart is finally ready for presentation and is shown in the next screenshot:

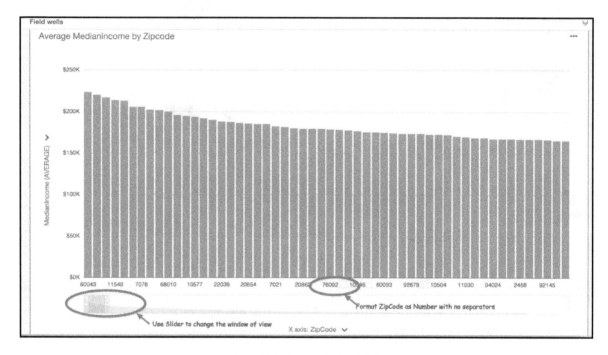

Figure 4.11: Median income by zip code final

This completes the creation of a new data analysis with simple bar chart visualization.

 Any changes to the new analysis are Auto saved by default. This can be changed with the option seen next to the analysis name called **Autosave ON**.

Renaming and adding descriptions to an existing analysis

We can rename an existing analysis by first selecting the desired analysis from the QuickSight home page and then editing the text next to analysis name. We can also add title and add description by clicking on the + add button to the left of the analysis name as shown in the following screenshot:

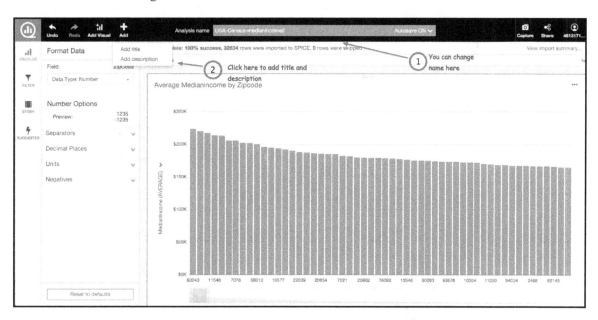

Figure 4.12: Rename analysis

This concludes the section for editing an existing analysis. Next let's check out how to delete an analysis.

Deleting an existing analysis

We can delete an existing analysis by first selecting the desired analysis from the QuickSight home page and then clicking on **Delete** as shown in the next screenshot.

You will be prompted for a confirmation. Click on **Delete** to complete the deletion.

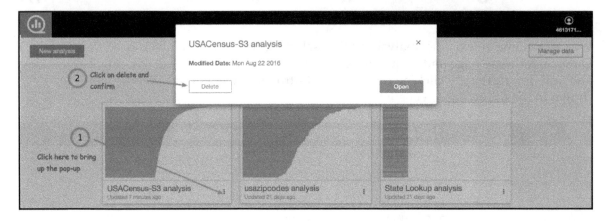

Figure 4.13: Deleting analysis

 Deleting the analysis does not delete the underlying dataset.

This concludes the section *Building analyses from datasets*; in the next section, we will review the best practices for selection of a chart type.

Building effective visuals

QuickSight visuals are interactive and support customization, sorting, and filters. In this section, we will see the different options and recommendations. The following are the options under QuickSight:

- Bar chart
- Line chart
- Pivot table
- Scatter plot
- Tree map
- Pie chart
- Heat map
- Autograph

Changing visual type

To change the current visual of a chart, follow the steps as follows:

1. Select the analysis you wish to change.
2. Next, expand the **Visual types** section and you will see all available options as shown in the following screenshot:

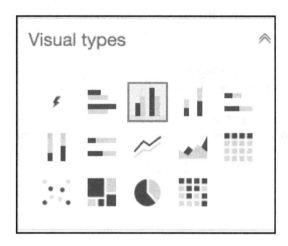

Figure 4.14: Visual types

3. Now you can select the chart you want to change to.
4. Alternatively, you can select the autograph option, which is represented by the lightning sign. QuickSight will use the most appropriate visual type based on the dataset.

Bar charts

QuickSight supports a wide range of bar charts for single-measure, multi-measure, stacked, or stacked 100% in horizontal or vertical orientation. In the next few sections we will discuss how to best use bar charts.

Simple bar charts

For single/multi measures against one dimension, select the simple bar chart, either horizontal or vertical. Let's see an example of multi-measure bar charts with the USA-Census-S3-DataSet:

1. Select the visualization type: horizontal bar charts.
2. Select measures and dimension fields. The best way to set them is to use the **Field wells** options, as shown in the following screenshot identified with the number **3**.
3. Format the columns for sorting, currency, format, decimal places, and units as desired.
4. Optionally, change the display range by dragging and/or moving the selected window as identified by **5** in the following screenshot:

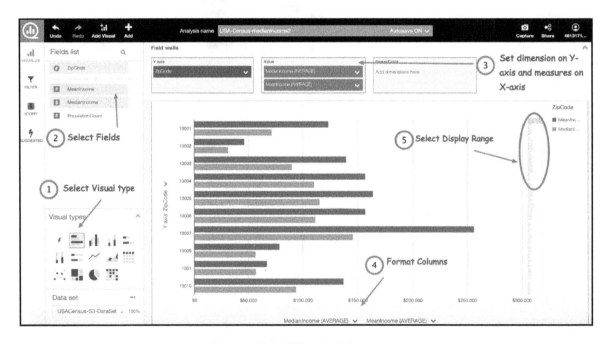

Figure 4.15: Simple bar chart

This completes the creation of a simple horizontal bar chart.

Stacked bar charts

For metrics that have several categories, you can use stacked bar charts. To explain this, we will use the AWS cost, usage, and report data that has details on where the AWS dollars were spent for your account.

 To enable AWS cost, usage, and report data to automatically extract and upload to your S3 account, refer to this link `https://aws.amazon.com/ab out-aws/whats-new/2016/08/aws-cost-and-usage-report-data-is-no w-easy-to-upload-directly-into-amazon-redshift-and-amazon-quic ksight/`.

Let's look at the steps to build a useful stacked horizontal bar chart showing the unblended cost aggregated by hour, grouped by the AWS service code as shown in the next screenshot:

1. Select the visualization type: vertical stacked bar chart.
2. Select measures, dimension, and group fields. The best way to set them is to use the **Field wells** options as shown in the following screenshot, identified with the number 3. The **Group/Color** field should be the category.
3. Next, format the columns for sorting, currency, format, separator decimal places, and time aggregation (hour in this case) as shown in the following screenshot:

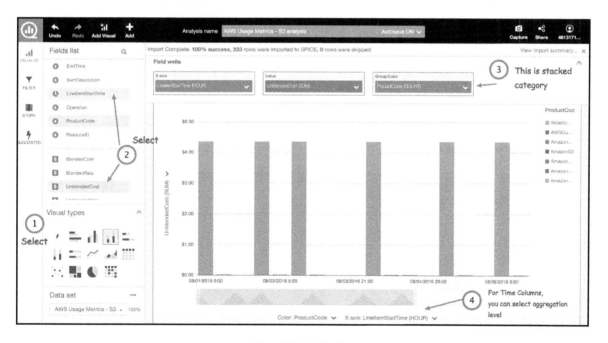

Figure 4.16: Stacked bar chart

This completes the stacked bar chart creation. To use a scale based on 100% instead of the value, select the vertical 100% bar chart option. The resultant chart is shown in the following screenshot:

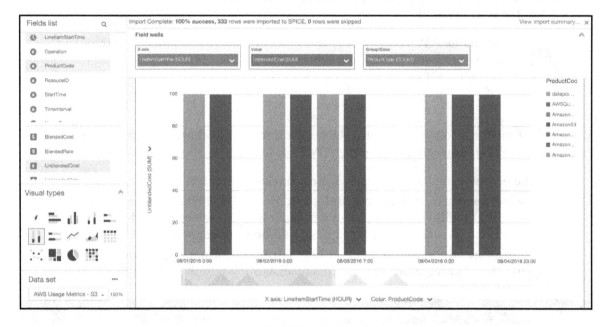

Figure 4.17: Stacked bar with 100% option

Line charts

Line charts are a great way to visualize trends of multiple metrics over a period time. QuickSight provides two types of line charts – simple line and area line chart. Let's review them with an example.

Simple line chart

We can use a line chart to compare values for one or more measures over a period of time. To create a line chart with cost and rate aggregated on a daily basis, follow the steps as follows:

1. Select the visualization type: line chart.
2. Select time-based field for X-axis and measures for values. The best way to set them is to use the **Field wells** options, as shown in the following screenshot identified with the number **3**.
3. Next, format the columns for sorting, currency, format, separator decimal places, and time aggregation (day in this case) as shown in the following screenshot:

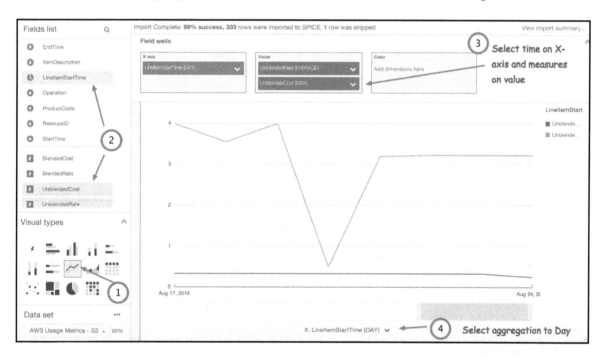

Figure 4.18: Simple line chart

4. Optionally, you can create a multi-dimension chart by selecting one measure as value and one field for dimension. For example, if we want to see `UnblendedCost` by various product codes in the preceding dataset, you will get a chart as shown in the following screenshot:

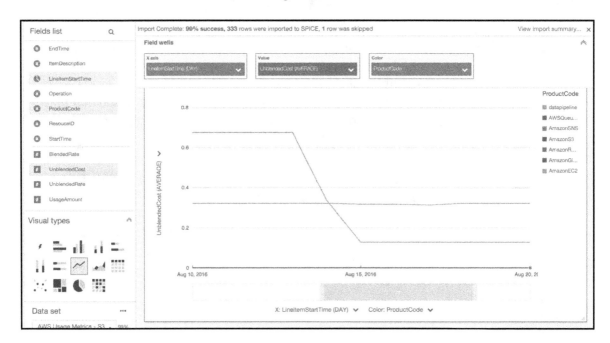

Figure 4.19: Line chart multiple dimension

 When selecting multiple dimension line charts, only one measure can be reported as a value.

Area line chart

Area line charts can also be used to compare one or more measures over time like the simple line chart; the key difference is the appearance; here a colored area instead of a line represents each value.

Let's review the steps to create an area line chart with cost and rate aggregated on a daily basis; following are the steps:

1. Select the visualization type as area line chart.
2. Select time-based field for *X*-axis and measures for values. The best way to set them is to use the **Field wells** options, as shown in the following screenshot identified with the number **3**.
3. Next, format the columns for sorting, currency, format, separator decimal places, and time aggregation (day in this case) as shown in the following screenshot:

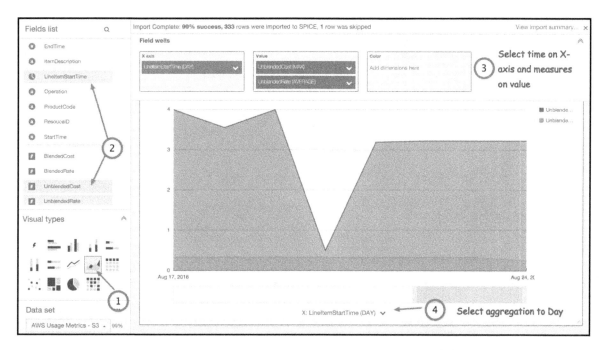

Figure 4.20: Area line chart

Pivot tables

Pivot tables are great for those who want to slice and dice measures across different dimensions in pure number form. Pivot tables allow sorting and statistical functions for further analysis. Let's review the steps to create a pivot table for sum of cost and rate grouped by, first, the date of service and then by the product.

1. Select the visualization type as pivot table.

2. Select time and product as the rows and measures rate and cost as values. The best way to set them is to use the **Field wells** options, as shown in the following screenshot identified with the number **3**.

3. This will populate the pivot table. Optionally sort the computed measures if needed.

4. The final chart is shown in the following screenshot:

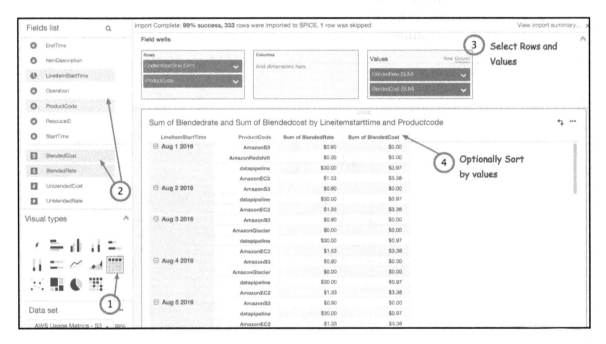

Figure 4.21: Pivot table

Adding statistical functions

Optionally, to the pivot table, we can add statistical functions like running total, and percentage of table to the pivot table cells. Following are the functions that are available in calculations:

- **Running total**: This gives the sum of a given cell value and values of all cells prior to it
- **Difference**: This gives the difference of a given cell and the immediate prior cell
- **Percentage difference**: This gives the difference between a cell value and the value of the cell prior to it divided by the value of the cell prior to it

- **Rank**: This provides the rank of the cell value compared to the values of other cells
- **Percentile**: This provides the percent of the values that are at or below the value for the given cell

To select the statistical function for a value, click on the right side of the value that brings up a pop-up and then select **Add table calculation** as shown in the following screenshot:

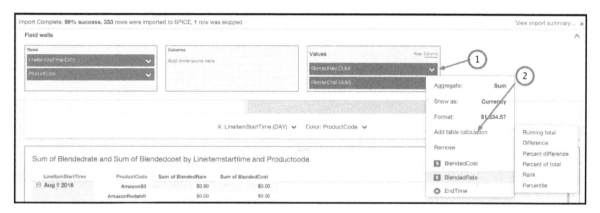

Figure 4.22: Pivot table statistical options

The calculations can be applied in one of the following ways:

- **Table across**: The calculation applies across the columns of the pivot table. This is the default
- **Table down**: The calculation applies down the rows of the pivot table
- **Table across down**: The calculation applies across the columns and then down the rows of the pivot table
- **Table down across**: The calculation applies down the rows and then across the columns of the pivot table
- **Group across**: The calculation applies across the columns of the pivot table, with subtotals by group
- **Group down**: The calculation applies down the rows of the pivot table, with subtotals by group
- **Group across down**: The calculation applies across the columns and then down the rows of the pivot table, with subtotals by group
- **Group down across**: The calculation applies down the rows and then across the columns of the pivot table, with subtotals by group

The following screenshot shows how to access these menu options for a given calculated function:

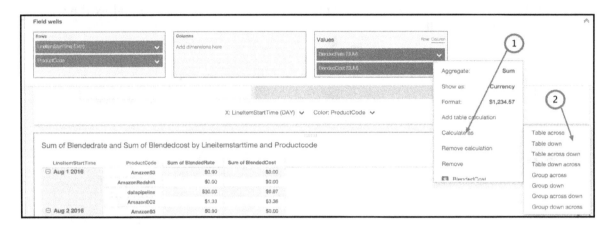

Figure 4.23: Pivot table statistical function selection

This completes usage of pivot tables. Now let's review how to build and use scatter plots.

Scatter plot

Scatter plots are a great way to visualize two or three measures for a dimension. Let's take an example for visualizing the USA census data and see how a scatter plot allows quick analysis of two measures: median income and population count for the zip code dimension.

Following are the steps to create a scatter plot:

1. Select the visualization type as scatter plot.
2. Select **PopulationCount** as measure for **X axis**, **MedianIncome** as measure for **Y axis**, **ZipCode** as the dimension for **Group/Color** of the bubbles and **MeanIncome** as size of bubble. The best way to set them is to use the **Field wells** options, as shown in the following screenshot identified with the number **3**.
3. Next, format the measures and dimensions for currency and number respectively.
4. This will populate the scatter plot as shown in the next screenshot.

5. A scatter plot cannot be sorted.

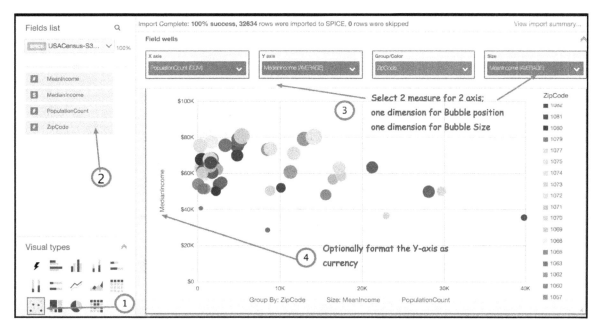

Figure 4.24: Scatter plot

 You must use aggregation for measures in the **X axis**, **Y axis**, **Size**, or **Field wells**, and cannot apply aggregation to the dimension you choose for the **Group/Color**.

This completes usage of a scatter plot. Now let's review how to build and use tree maps.

Tree map

Tree maps are another intuitive visualization for one or more measures against a single dimension. It is a graphic that has a collage of several rectangles where each rectangle size represents the proportion of the value for that item to the whole of the dimension for the selected measure. Rectangles also have color-coding for easily differentiating the values for the measure with darker colors indicating higher values and lighter colors indicating lower values.

Let's take an example for visualizing the USA census data and see how a tree map allows quick analysis of two measures: median income and population count for the zip code dimension.

Following are the steps to create a tree map chart:

1. Select the visualization type as tree map.
2. Select **PopulationCount** as measure **Size** of the blocks, **MedianIncome** as measure for color, and **ZipCode** as the dimension for grouping. The best way to set them is to use the **Field wells** options, as shown in the following screenshot identified with the number **3**.
3. Next, format the measures and dimension for currency and number respectively.
4. This will populate the tree map as shown in the following screenshot:

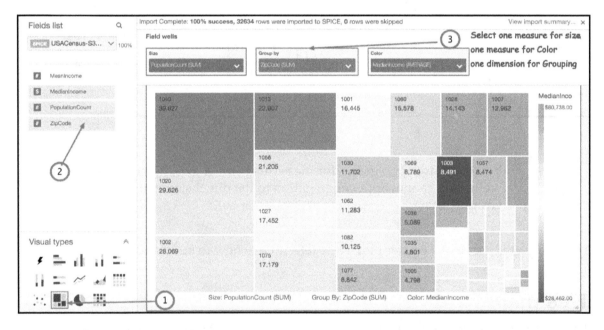

Figure 4.25: Tree map

This completes usage of a tree map. Now let's review how to build and use pie charts.

Pie chart

Pie charts are another popular charting option for a single measure and dimension where the graph is a circle which is divided into several slices. Each slice/wedge in a pie chart represents the proportion of the value for the item to the whole. Let's take an example for visualizing the USA census data and see how the measure population count is visualized by zip code. Following are the steps to create a pie chart:

1. Select the visualization type as pie chart.
2. Select **PopulationCount** as value and **ZipCode** as the dimension for grouping. The best way to set them is to use the **Field wells** options, as shown in the following screenshot identified with the number **3**.
3. Next, format the measures and dimensions for currency and number respectively.
4. This will populate the pie chart as shown in the following screenshot:

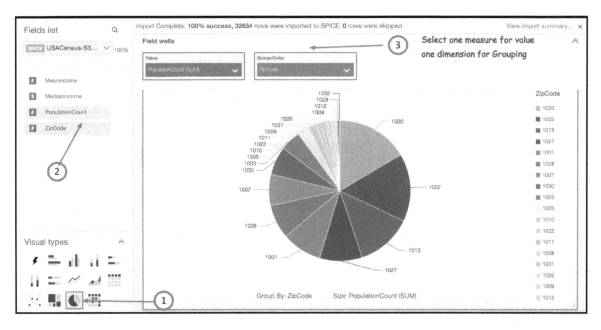

Figure 4.26: Pie chart

This completes usage of pie charts. Now let's review how to build and use heat maps.

Heat map

A heat map shows a measure in a table format where each cell is an intersection of two dimensions in color. The color-coding easily differentiates the values for the measure with darker colors indicating higher values and lighter colors indicating lower values.

Let's take an example for visualizing the AWS usage metrics and see the measure usage amount in seconds for every intersection of operations and time (rounded to hours). Following are the steps to create a heat map:

1. Select the visualization type as heat map.
2. Select **Operation** as the dimension for **Rows**, **LineItemStartTime** for **Columns** and **UsageAmount** measure for the **Values**. The best way to set them is to use the **Field wells** options, as shown in the following screenshot identified with the number **3**.
3. Next, set the aggregation for values as sum (you can select other options if you desire).
4. This will populate the heat map as shown in the following screenshot:

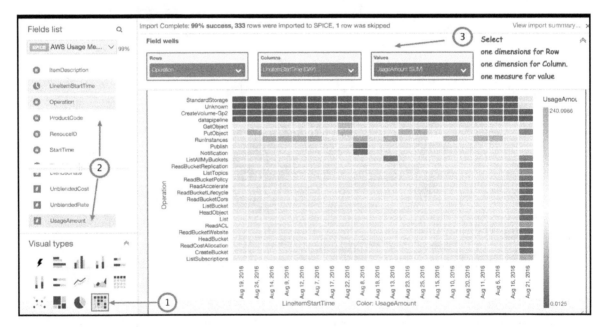

Figure 4.27: Heat map

This completes all standard chart selections. Now let's review how to use autograph feature.

Autograph

Autograph is a great feature when you are experimenting with a new dataset and want QuickSight to automatically figure out which visual type will work best for the data. Let's see the steps for this feature using the **AWS Usage Metrics** dataset.

1. Select the lightning icon from the **Visual types**.
2. Next, select **UnblendedCost** and **Operation** field and see the chart automatically get created as shown in the following screenshot:

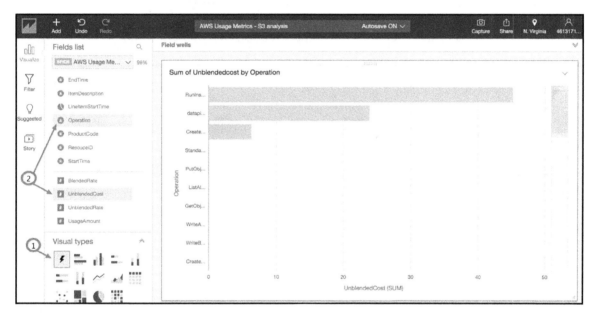

Figure 4.28: Autograph

3. In this scenario, autograph selected a horizontal bar chart with the highest cost operation shown on top.

This completes the autograph section. Next we will review general configuration and options to improve appearance.

General options

In this section, we will review some options to personalize and enhance the look and feel of your visual.

Configuring the visual title

The visual title is displayed by default. Use the following steps to modify the title:

1. From the analysis page, select the visual you want to format.
2. Next, on the right side of the visual you will see a **v** sign, which when clicked will show the **Format Visual** pane on the left as shown in the following screenshot:

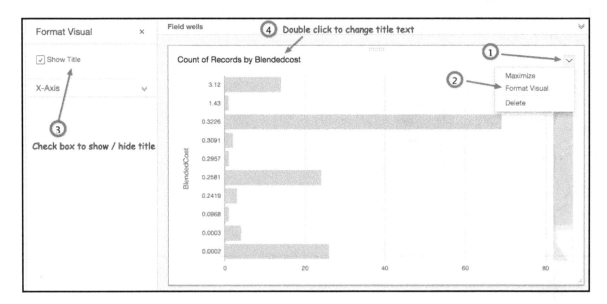

Figure 4.29: Visual formatting options

3. On the left-hand side, QuickSight shows details on what formatting options are allowed; for title you can turn on/off. If you want to change the title text, just double-click on the title and change the text.

Configuring legends

By default, QuickSight will display the legend. Use the following steps to hide the legend or change its position:

1. From the analysis page, select the visual you want to format.
2. Next, on the right side of the visual you will see a **v** sign, which when clicked will show the **Format Visual** pane on the left as shown in the following screenshot:

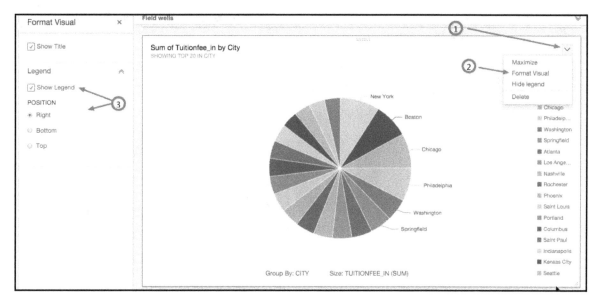

Figure 4.30: Legend changes

3. Now you will see legend configuration options on the left-hand side that can hide the legend or move it to the right/bottom/top of the visual.

Configuring the axis range

By default, the axis range starts at zero and ends near the highest value of the measure being displayed; if you want to modify the steps proceed as follows:

1. From the analysis page, select the visual you want to format.
2. Next, on the right side of the visual you will see a **v** sign, which when clicked will show the **Format Visual** pane on the left as shown in the following screenshot:

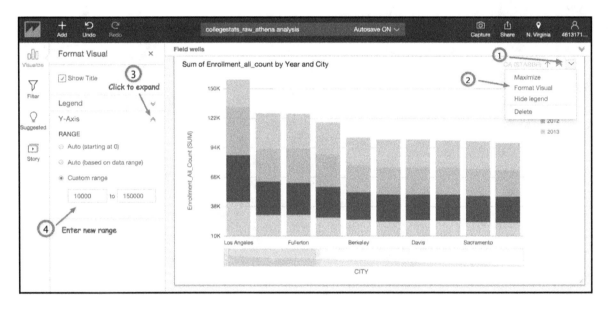

Figure 4.31: Formatting axis

3. On the left-hand side you will see the **Format Visual** pane, which has the axis range settings. Here you can change the range to auto, based on data range, or a **Custom range** as shown in the preceding screenshot, `10000` to `150000`.
4. The chart automatically updates itself to the new range.

 For horizontal charts, you can configure the X-axis, for vertical charts you can configure the Y-axis and for scatter plots you can configure both axes.

This completes the section for axis configuration, next we will review how to change colors.

Changing visual colors

QuickSight allows you to change the default colors. Use the following steps to change the colors of your charts:

1. From the analysis page, select the visual you want to format.
2. Next, choose any element on the visual to get the various properties for the chart, which will also have the option to change **Chart Color** as shown in the next screenshot.
3. In the example shown in the screenshot we have a stacked vertical bar; you can change the chart color for a specific year or for all years.

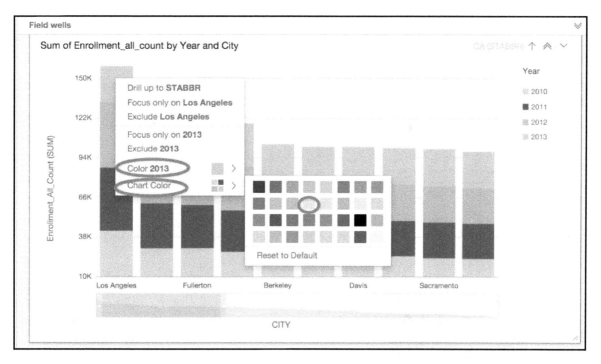

Figure 4.32: Changing colors

4. Let's repeat this for all years and see the resultant chart as shown here:

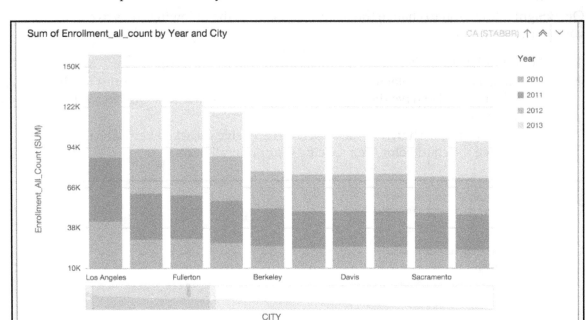

Figure 4.33: Updated colors on chart

This completes the section for configuring colors. Next we will review how to enhance charts with drill downs.

Adding drill down to charts

Certain datasets have hierarchies, and the charts will really be live if one can start from the summary and then drill down to details. For example, for the college enrollment data, we have information at the city level along with the states that they belong to; follow the steps to see how the chart drill down can be configured from the state to city level.

1. First, let's review the chart without drill down. The chart has the visual type of vertical stacked bar chart with X **axis** as **stateabbr** (state abbreviation), value as sum of enrollment, and group by as year as shown in the following screenshot:

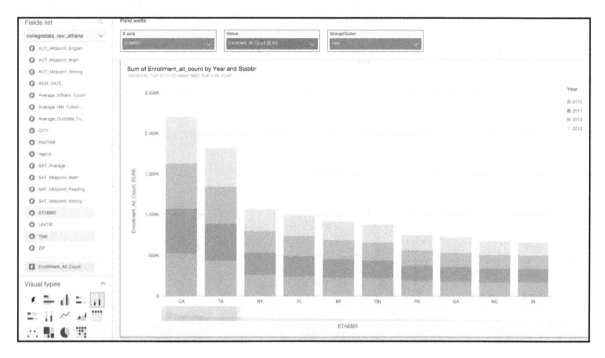

Figure 4.34: State level report without drill down

2. Now expand the **Field wells** pane and then drag the **CITY** field from the left **Fields list** to the **X axis** below the **STABBR** field. Make sure that, when you drag the field, you select **Add drill-down layer** and do not select the **Replace** option. You should see **City** below the **STABBR**. The following screenshot shows these steps in detail:

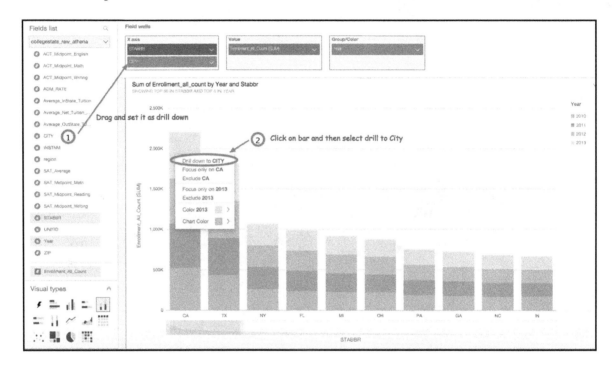

Figure 4.35: Drill down configuration

3. Now when you click on the vertical bar for the state of CA, you should see an option to drill down to **CITY**. When you click on that drill option, you will see the chart refresh with data shown for cities for the state of CA as shown in the next screenshot:

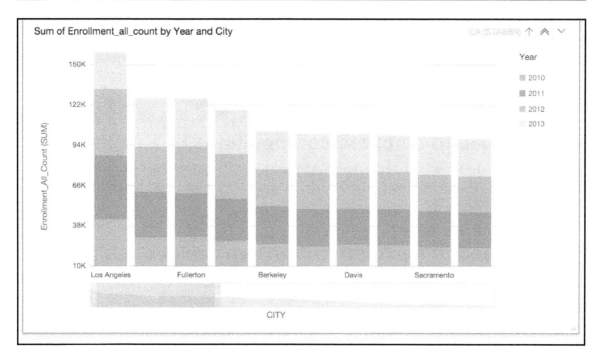

Figure 4.36: Drill down to city

 At this time, drill down is not available for pivot tables.

This completes the general formatting options for visuals in QuickSight; next, we will review guidelines on selecting the right kind of visuals based on your needs.

Selecting the right visualizations

Choosing the right amount of data and chart type is crucial for effective visualization and reporting. First, one should know what questions the business would ask about the data. Next, there are certain recommended charts based on the patterns of these responses.

Does the business want to compare values?

Let's say the need is to compare revenue over time, or to compare customer counts by different states in the country. For such use cases, select horizontal bar, vertical bar, or line charts.

Do you need to compare compositions of a measure?

Let's say we have a need to show revenue by region and also show the various product categories constituting the sales in the region. For such use cases, select horizontal stacked bar or vertical stacked bar.

Do you need to see distributions and relationship between two measures?

Let's say we have a need to see the relationship between two measures like population median salary and crime rate. For such use cases, select scatter plot which will be useful for understanding the safest cities and the median salary. Other alternatives for such a question are tree map and heat map.

Do you want to see trends with multiple measures?

If you have a need to see trending of multiple measures over time, choose Line charts simple or area type. For example, consider a scenario where you want to see the increase/decrease of crime along with increase/decrease of overall population for the last 5 years.

Do you want to slice and dice multiple measures over different dimensions?

If you have a need to summarize, analyze, and present numbers based on different dimensions, pivot tables are an excellent option. For example, if you want to report sales metrics by product category and geographical region and for different years, you can pivot with rows representing geography (like states of the USA), columns being product category, and the intersection of each row and column being the actual metrics. Pivot tables also support sub-totals to help the analysis.

Deleting a visual

To delete an existing visual from an analysis is pretty simple, you first select the analysis and then click on the ellipses (**...**) next to the visual you want to delete and then click on the **Delete** menu. See the following screenshot that shows the **Delete** option:

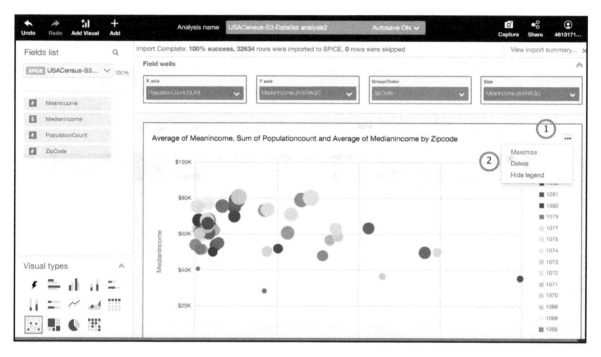

Figure 4.37: Deleting a visual

Telling a story

Story is an exciting feature from QuickSight that can be used for effective presentations and snapshots of your analysis that you want to share with your team members or executive management. QuickSight allows you to take a snapshot of your chart and preserve all the formatting and filters to what is called a **scene**. A story is a set of scenes that can be played in a sequence. In this section, we will review how to create and manage stories.

Creating a story

Every analysis comes with a default story called **Storyboard1**. As you work with your analysis, you can capture a specific visual to the **StoryBoard** as a scene. Let's review the steps to create a story using the USA census analysis.

1. From the QuickSight home page, select the **USA Census** analysis.
2. Next, select the first chart that you want to add to the **Story** and click on **Capture** in the top-right corner.
3. This will change the focus of the toolbar from **Visualize** to **Story**.
4. Next, you can rename the scene from **Scene 1** to **Bubble Chart**.
5. You can optionally rename the default **Storyboard1** to a new name, for example **USA Census Storyboard** as shown in the following screenshot:

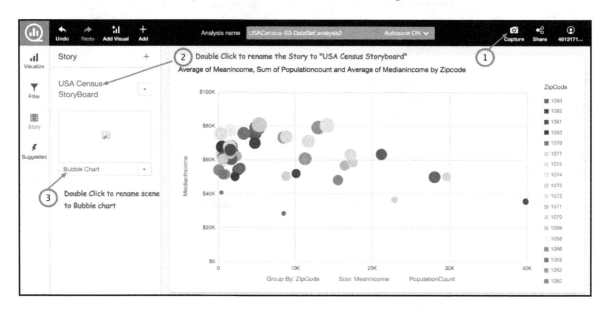

Figure 4.38: Story creation

6. Next, let's add two more scenes to this story with the heat map and pie chart by clicking the **Capture** option again.

7. Now you have a **Story** with three scenes as shown in the following screenshot:

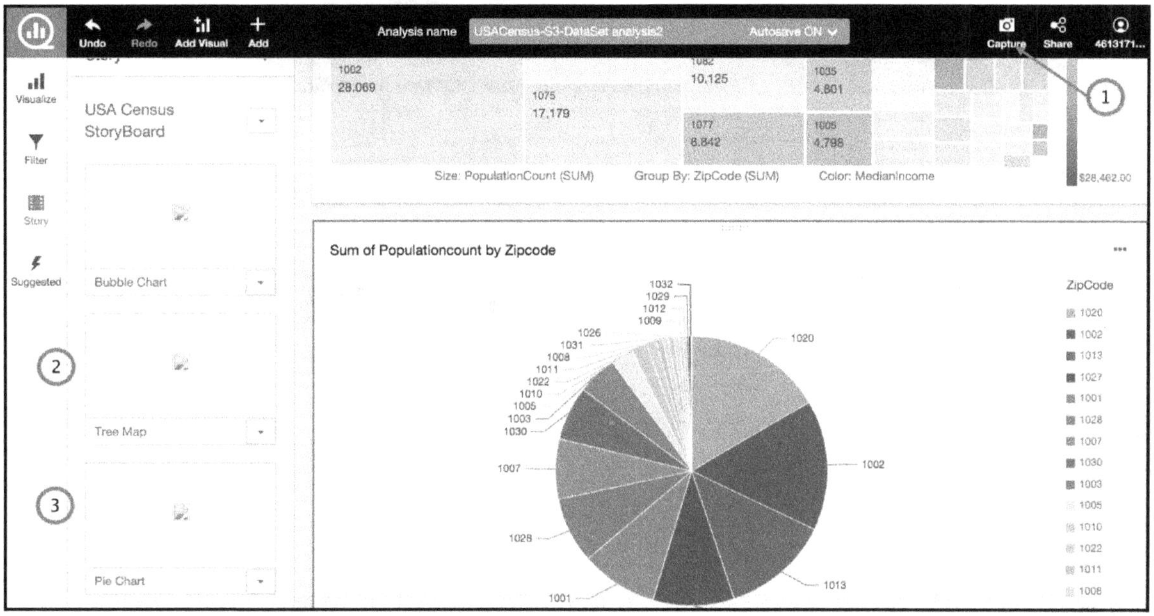

Figure 4.39: Story creation additional chart

This completes the section for the creation of a new story. Next we will review how to play existing stories.

Playing a Story

Let's review the steps to play an existing story:

1. From the QuickSight home page, select the **USA Census** analysis.
2. Next, click on the **Story** button from the toolbar on the left side.

3. Next, hover over the first scene and the play icon will appear at the center; click on the play sign as shown in the following screenshot:

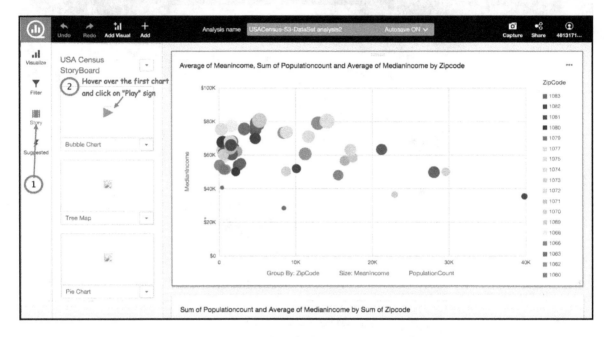

Figure 4.40: Play a story

4. This starts the story in play mode; you can use the **NEXT** and/or **PREVIOUS** button on the bottom to move forward or go back to the previous scene as shown in the next screenshot.

5. Once you are done with the story presentation, click on the **Stop** button to exist the story view mode.

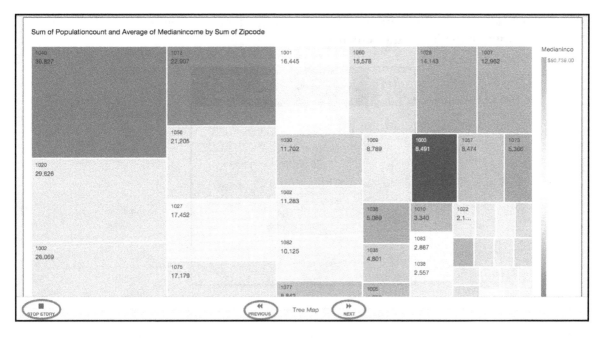

Figure 4.41: Controls for a story

Deleting a Story

Follow the steps to delete an existing story:

1. From the QuickSight home page, select the **USA Census** analysis.
2. Next, click on the **Story** button from the tool bar on the left side.
3. Next, click on the dropdown next to the story name.

4. Click on the **Delete** option in the drop-down menu to finally delete the story as shown in the following screenshot:

Figure 4.42: Delete story

This completes the section on stories. Next we will look into the dashboard feature.

Sharing dashboards

A read-only snapshot of an analysis can be shared with other QuickSight users by using dashboards. The users who are given access to the dashboard can view and filter the dashboard data, and re-share the dashboard with others.

Following are the steps for creating and publishing a dashboard:

1. From the QuickSight home page, select the **USA Census** analysis
2. Next, click on the **Share** button from the application bar and then select **Create new dashboard** as an option.
3. Enter a name for the dashboard.

4. Next, click on **Create dashboard** as shown in the following screenshot:

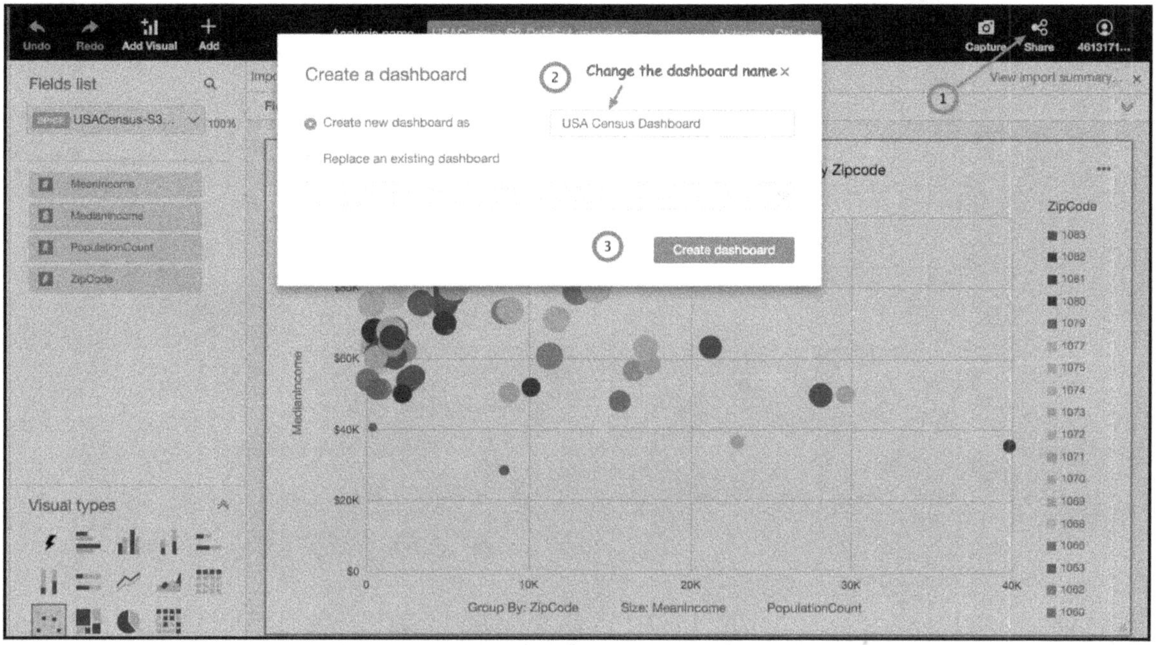

Figure 4.43: Dashboard creation

5. Next, you can publish to other QuickSight users by entering username or e-mails as shown in the following screenshot.

6. And finally, click on **Publish Dashboard** to publish and share the dashboard.

Figure 4.44: Publishing a dashboard

Deleting a dashboard

You can delete a dashboard that you have published using the following steps:

1. From the QuickSight home page, click on **All dashboards** tab.
2. Next, for the dashboard you want to delete, click on the **...** on the extreme bottom right which will pop-up a new window for that dashboard.
3. In the pop-up, you will see the option to delete the dashboard as shown in the following screenshot.

4. Next, you will get a final confirmation to delete the dashboard.

Figure 4.45: Deleting dashboard

Summary

QuickSight provides a wide range of graphics to effectively analyze your data. The typical workflow to create insights is to first create datasets in QuickSights from sources like S3; then, prepare data; next create, QuickSight analysis, and then add visuals to analysis. For a given analysis, you can select one or more visualization options such as bar charts, lines charts, pivot tables, scatter plots, tree maps, pie charts, or heat maps.

QuickSight provides a storyboarding feature that can be used to preserve snapshots of an analysis and re-play the visuals in sequence as scenes of the Story. QuickSight also has a dashboard feature that can be used to share a read-only snapshot of an analysis to other QuickSight users.

However, QuickSight does lag behind its competitors in the feature set for visualizations and I expect, in future releases, it will enhance these capabilities.

In the next chapter, we will see how to manage users in QuickSight and manage permissions granted to QuickSight on AWS resources to secure your environment.

5
Secure Your Environment

To secure your BI environment, you need to control which users have access to QuickSight and also what resources QuickSight has permissions to read. In this chapter, we will review the following in detail:

- Managing users and access

- Managing QuickSight permissions on AWS resources

- Authorizing connections from QuickSight to RDS and Redshift instances

- Authorizing connections from QuickSight to EC2 instances

Managing users and access

There are two types of users supported by QuickSight: the first type of user is the AWS **IAM** (**Identity and Access Management**) user and the second type is the user managed completely within QuickSight. If your enterprise has IAM-managed users, this is the recommended approach since IAM enables the admin to securely control access to all AWS services and resources, including QuickSight.

For a QuickSight standard edition account, you can set up up to 100 user accounts, including the root account used to create the QuickSight account. To increase this limit, you can raise an AWS service limit request by opening a support case with AWS support.

To manage users, you must have administrator privileges. Let's review how to add, reactivate, and delete users.

Adding new users

To invite others to your QuickSight account, you just need a valid e-mail address or IAM user account name.

User account creation is a two-step process: first you send an invitation to join, which creates an inactive user in QuickSight and sends them an e-mail. Next, after the user accepts the invitation and signs up to QuickSight, their account is activated.

Follow these steps to add new users:

1. From the QuickSight home page, click on the far-right person icon, which will bring down a menu.
2. Select the **Manage QuickSight** option from the menu and then select **Manage Users** from the left-hand side menu, as shown in the following screenshot:

Figure 5.1: Manage QuickSight

3. This will bring up the following user management screen, where you can invite additional users and/or delete existing users:

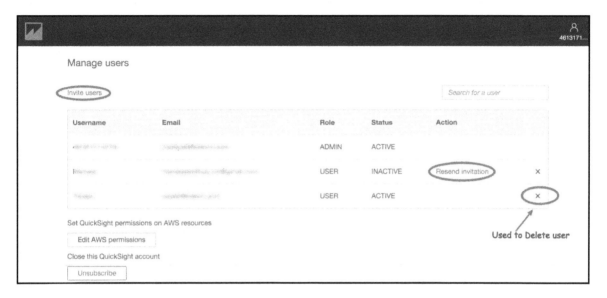

Figure 5.2: User management

4. In the next popup, you can invite a user by their IAM username or e-mail address.
5. Next, select the role **Admin/User** from the dropdown as shown in the next screenshot.

6. You can invite multiple users using this popup and click on the **Invite** button once you are done.

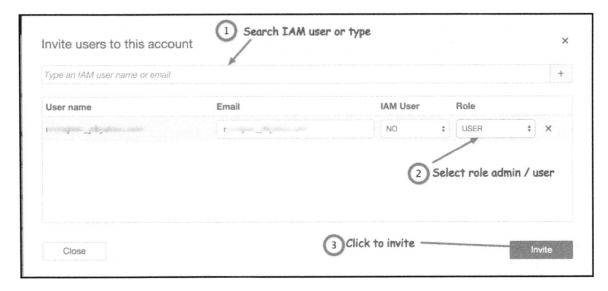

Figure 5.3: Invite new user

 When creating an IAM admin user, you need to ensure that the user has all the necessary statements in their IAM permissions policy to work with QuickSight resources.

This completes the adding users section; now, let's review how to reactivate a user.

Reactivate a user

If the user is sent an invitation and they don't respond within 24 hours, the invitation will expire and the user account in QuickSight will remain in inactive status. You can do the following steps to resend the invitation:

1. From the QuickSight home page, select **Manage QuickSight** and then **Manage Users** from the left-hand side menu.
2. Next you will see the list of users with their status **Active/Inactive**. If the list is long, use the search for a user to filter down the user list.
3. You can click on the link **Resend Invitation** for the inactive user/s.
4. Click on **Confirm**.

This will resend the invitation, and now the users have another 24 hours to accept and activate their QuickSight account.

View existing User

After a user is created and you want to check details about their account, you can use the following steps to view the account details:

1. From the QuickSight home page, select **Manage QuickSight** and then **Manage Users** from the left-hand side menu.
2. You can now browse the list of all users or locate a specific user by typing the first few characters of that account name or e-mail address. QuickSight will show you the matching results, as shown in the next screenshot. The search is case insensitive and wildcards are not supported.

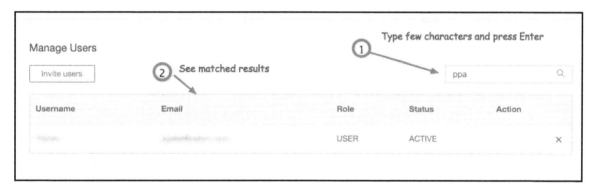

Figure 5.4: View and search users

The preceding steps will provide details of the user, including e-mail address, account status, and role in QuickSight.

Deleting a user

If you wish to delete an existing user, you can follow these steps:

1. From the QuickSight home page, select **Manage QuickSight**.
2. Next you will see the list of users with an **X** at the end of each entry.

3. Upon clicking on the **X**, you will be prompted to either transfer all resources owned by that user to another account or delete all the linked resources, as shown here:

Figure 5.5: Delete account confirmation

4. If you chose to transfer the resources, enter the username of the account you want to transfer to and then choose **Delete and transfer resources**.
5. If you chose to delete all resources, click on the **Delete** option.

The user account is now deleted from your QuickSight account.

Enterprise account user management

If you have a QuickSight enterprise edition, you can add multiple users to QuickSight by choosing one or more Microsoft AD directory groups. All enterprise accounts have no user limits. In this section, we will review the steps add AD users to QuickSight.

Prerequisites

Before you get started with AD integration with QuickSight, your AWS account needs the following AWS permissions:

```
ds:DescribeTrusts
quicksight:GetGroupMapping
quicksight:SearchDirectoryGroups
quicksight:SetGroupMapping
```

Adding AD user accounts to QuickSight

We can add multiple user accounts at once by selecting one or more Microsoft AD directory groups to integrate with QuickSight. You can also add AD users individually if you want to manage a smaller list. The following are the steps to add an AD directory group to QuickSight:

1. From the QuickSight home page, click on the far-right person icon, which will bring down a menu.
2. Select the **Manage QuickSight** option from the menu, select **Manage Users**, and then choose **Manage Groups**.
3. Next, on the AWS sign-in page, enter your AWS or IAM user and password.
4. Now you can search or type the AD group name under either administration groups or user groups depending on the privileges you want the group members to have. For example, you can have a data-engineer AD group in the administration role and the ad hoc-user AD group in the user role.
5. Click on **Add selected groups** and now all users in those groups will get access to QuickSight.

Deactivating AD accounts with QuickSight

We can deactivate one or more Microsoft AD directory groups from integration with Amazon QuickSight. All users in the selected groups will then be deactivated from QuickSight. Optionally you can deactivate specific users instead of the entire group. Follow these steps to remove an AD directory group from QuickSight:

1. From the QuickSight home page, click on the far-right person icon, which will bring down a menu.
2. Select the **Manage QuickSight** option from the menu and then select **Manage Users**. Then choose **Manage Groups**.
3. Next, on the AWS sign-in page, enter your AWS or IAM user and password.
4. You can now search the AD group or browse it.
5. Then click on the remove icon next to the group to deactivate it from QuickSight.

This completes the enterprise account user management specifically with Microsoft AD groups. Next, we will review how to manage permissions to AWS resources so that QuickSight can report on it.

Managing QuickSight permissions on AWS resources

You can control the permissions given to QuickSight to access your AWS resources using the following steps:

1. From the QuickSight home page, select **Manage QuickSight**.
2. Next, click on **Account Permissions** from the left-hand side menu and then click on the **Edit AWS permissions** button as shown in the screenshot here:

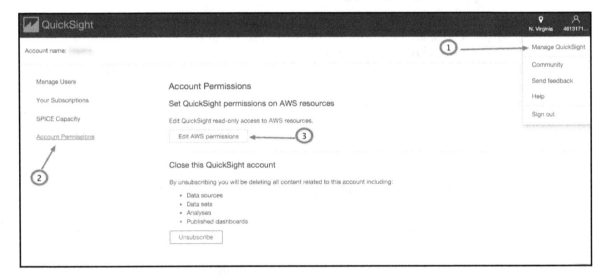

Figure 5.6: AWS permissions

3. This will show **Edit QuickSight read-only access to AWS resources** page as shown in the next screenshot. From here, you can select Enable auto discovery of your data and users in AWS Redshift, RDS and IAM services and enable/disable access to AWS resources:

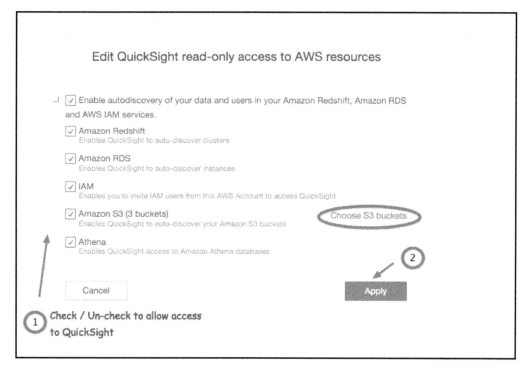

Figure 5.7: AWS permission checks

4. For the S3 buckets, you can click on **Choose S3 buckets** and further control which buckets you want QuickSight to have access to. You will see a popup like the one shown next. If you make any changes, click on **Select buckets** and then **Apply** to preserve those changes.

5. If you have an Athena database, check the box for Athena to allow QuickSight to access them. You also need to ensure that QuickSight has access to the S3 buckets used by Athena.

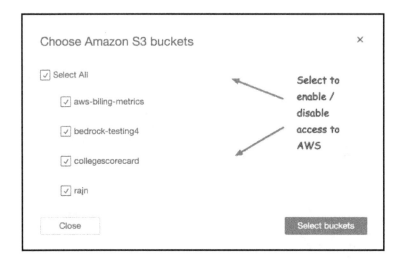

Figure 5.8: AWS S3 buckets permission

After you make changes, do remember to click on **Apply**. This completes managing QuickSight permissions on AWS resources.

Authorizing connections from QuickSight to AWS data sources

Amazon QuickSight servers need access to RDS instances and Redshift clusters that you want it to connect to. In the next few sections, we will see how to enable these connections to QuickSight.

Creating a new security group for QuickSight

It is a good practice to have a separate security group that can enable QuickSight to access RDS instances, Redshift, and EC2 instances. In this section we will look into the steps for creating this new security group.

At the time this book was authored, the IP range for QuickSight servers was 52.23.63.224/27. This CIDR block is reserved for QuickSight in the US east (North Virginia) region.

Use the following steps to create a new security group with permissions to QuickSight:

1. From the AWS services listing, select the **VPC** service, which can also be accessed by using this URL: https://console.aws.amazon.com/vpc/. From here, click on **Security Groups** and then on the **Create Security Group** button as shown here:

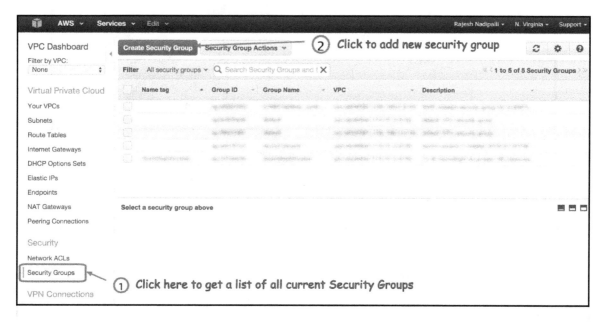

Figure 5.9: Create new security group

2. This will result in a popup to create a new security group. Enter the **Name tag** as `QuickSightAccess`, **Group name** as `QuickSightAccess`, and a **Description** as shown in the next figure. Ensure that the VPC identifier is same as that of the RDS instance it is associated with. Once you are done, click on **Yes, Create**:

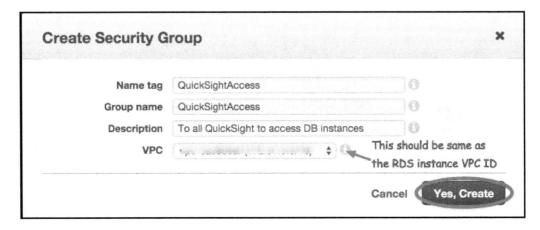

Figure 5.10: New security group

3. The new security group will have default settings with no inbound rules; click on **Edit** to configure this:

Figure 5.11: Inbound rules edit

4. Next set the new rule with **Type** as **Custom TCP Rule**, **Protocol** as **TCP (5)**, **Port Range** as appropriate for the RDS instances you want to be opened, and the source IP address range of the QuickSight servers `52.23.63.224/27`. This is shown in the following screenshot. Once you have filled it, click on **Save** to retain these changes:

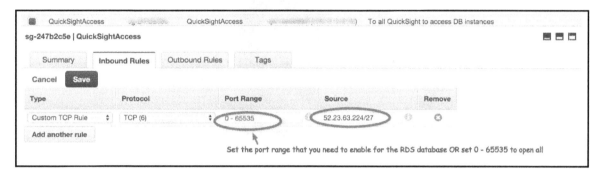

Figure 5.12: Inbound rules setup

This completes the setup of a separate security group for QuickSight.

Authorizing connections to RDS instances

For Amazon QuickSight to connect to RDS instances, you need to set the VPC that has inbound rule authorization access from the IP range of QuickSight servers created in the previous section *Creating a new security group for QuickSight*.

Use the following steps to enable QuickSight access to RDS instances:

1. First navigate to the RDS service and select the RDS instance that you wish to grant access to. You can use the following URL to get the RDS service: `https://c onsole.aws.amazon.com/rds`.

2. Next, click on **Instance Actions** and select **Modify** as shown in this screenshot:

Figure 5.13: Modify RDS instance

3. In the **Network & Security** section, select the newly created security group **QuickSightAccess** and then click on **Continue** to save the changes.

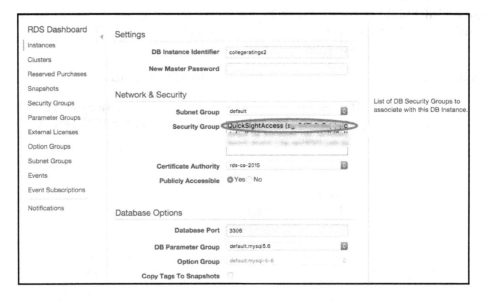

Figure 5.14: Associate QuickSight with RDS

4. Now, your RDS instance is set up correctly so that QuickSight can access it. You can validate this by going to the QuickSight **Manage data** page; select the RDS instance, add the username and password, and click on the **Validated** button, as shown here:

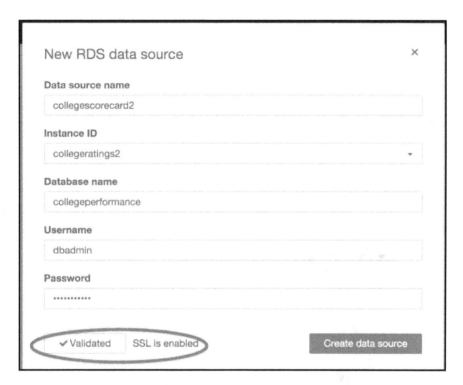

Figure 5.15: Validate RDS connectivity

Authorizing connections to Redshift cluster

For Amazon QuickSight to connect to Redshift cluster, you need to set the VPC that has inbound rule authorization access from the IP range of QuickSight servers created in the previous section, *Creating a new security group for QuickSight*.

Use the following steps to enable QuickSight access to Redshift cluster:

1. First navigate to the Redshift service page, which you can access using the URL: `https://console.aws.amazon.com/redshift/`.

2. From here, select the Redshift cluster you wish to grant access to, as shown in this screenshot:

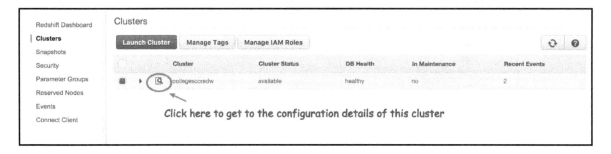

Figure 5.16: Redshift clusters

3. Next, you need to modify the cluster and select the VPC security group that **QuickSightAccess** created in the *Creating new security group for QuickSight* section. Finally click on the **Modify** button to preserve the changes, as shown here:

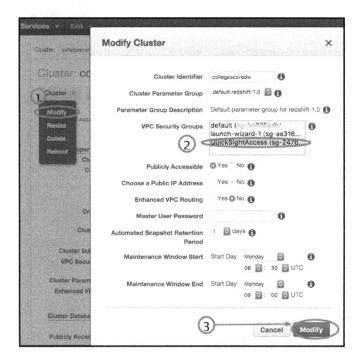

Figure 5.17: Modify Redshift

4. This completes the setup of the Redshift cluster for QuickSight; now let's verify that these changes are working by going to QuickSight home page and adding a new data source for this Redshift database:

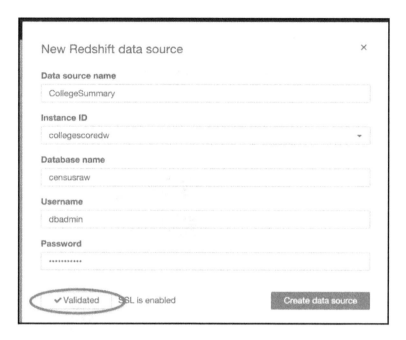

Figure 5.18: Redshift verification

This completes the Redshift setup so that QuickSight has access to it.

Authorizing connections to EC2 instance

For Amazon QuickSight to connect to EC2 instances, you need to set the VPC that has inbound rule authorization access from the IP range of QuickSight servers created in the previous section, *Creating a new security group for QuickSight*.

Use the following steps to enable QuickSight access to RDS instances:

1. First navigate to the EC2 Service at the following URL:
   `https://console.aws.amazon.com/ec2`.
2. Next, select the instance that you want to grant access to. Click on `Actions` and then **Networking**. Select **Change Security Groups** as shown in this screenshot:

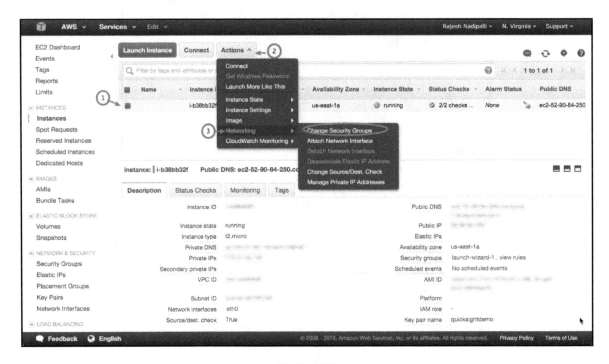

Figure 5.19: Select EC2 instance

3. Next, you will see a new page pop up with the various security groups; select **QuickSightAccess**, which we previously created, and click on **Assign Security Groups** as shown here:

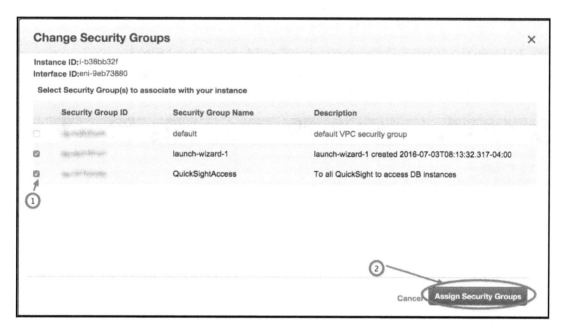

Figure 5.20: Change security groups for EC2

This completes the EC2 setup so that QuickSight has access to this box.

Closing a QuickSight account

If you want to really close your QuickSight account, you can do so by unsubscribing from this service. You must be signed in as the AWS root account that was used to create the QuickSight account and then follow these steps:

1. From the QuickSight home page, select **Manage QuickSight**.
2. Next, click on **Account Permissions** from the left menu and then click on the **Unsubscribe** button as shown in this screenshot:

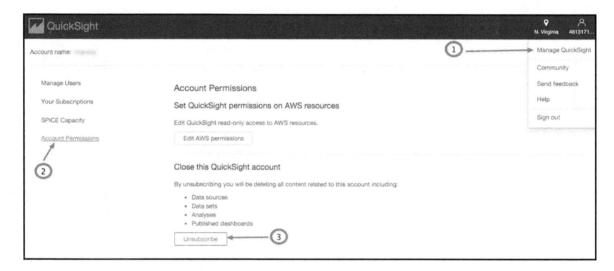

Figure 5.21: Unsubscribe account

3. This will now provide a warning page that unsubscribing will delete all related data sources, data sets, analyses, and dashboards. Click on **Unsubscribe** to finally confirm, as shown here:

Figure 5.22: QuickSight closing confirmation

This completes the closing of the QuickSight account.

Summary

As an architect or administrator, you need to plan out which users and which data sources you want QuickSight to have access to. To manage who has access, QuickSight administrators can manage user accounts, which can be IAM users or just any e-mail IDs. If you have an enterprise subscription, you can integrate a Microsoft AD account with QuickSight.

To manage permissions on what resources QuickSight should have access to, the administrator can do a blanket grant/revoke access from RDS instances, Redshift cluster, and selective S3 buckets. Additionally, for each RDS instance, Redshift cluster and/or EC2 instance that you wish to allow access to, you need to associate a new security group to authorize QuickSight servers using an address range. In future releases, the user management is expected to include IAM role-based access to simplify integration with other services.

In the next chapter, we will look into the QuickSight mobile application and see how the analyses created on the standard browser application can give you access in the palm of your hand.

6
QuickSight Mobile

The QuickSight mobile app allows you to stay connected to your data from anywhere, anytime, on your mobile devices. You can visualize, explore, and share your analyses, dashboards, and stories with an intuitive user experience. You can get answers to business questions in your hands and impress your peers and executives.

In this chapter, we will take an in-depth look at how this app works via the following topics:

- Installing the mobile app
- Accessing dashboards
- Accessing analyses
- Accessing stories
- Advanced options

Throughout this chapter we will reuse the analysis, dashboards, and stories that we built in Chapter 4, *Intuitive Visualizations*.

Installing QuickSight

Currently the QuickSight mobile application is only available for Apple devices with Android support coming soon. You can install the Amazon QuickSight app from the Apple iTunes store for no cost. You can search for the app from the iTunes store and then proceed to download and install, or alternatively you can follow this link to download the app: https://itunes.apple.com/us/app/amazon-quicksight/id1148226615?ls=1&mt=8.

Amazon QuickSight is certified to work with iOS devices running iOS Version 9.0 and above.

Once you have the app installed, you can proceed to log in to your QuickSight account, as shown in the following screenshot:

Figure 6.1: QuickSight sign in

After you log in to the application using a QuickSight account or an IAM account, it will show all dashboards and analyses that you have access to. On the mobile application, any changes you make such as changing the filters or chart type are done just for that session and not persisted to the original visuals so that you can explore without any worry.

Dashboards on the go

The first thing you will see in the QuickSight app is a list of dashboards that you are authorized to see with their respective links to a detailed view for easy access. If you don't see this dashboard list, then click on the **Dashboards** icon from the menu at the bottom of your mobile device, as shown in the following screenshot:

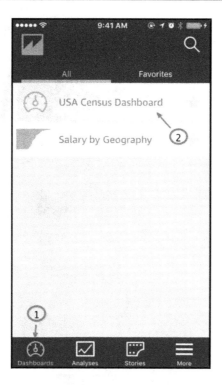

Figure 6.2: Accessing dashboards

You will now see the list of dashboards associated with your user ID. In the next few sections, we will review how to navigate to other dashboard features.

Dashboard detailed view

From the dashboard listing, select **USA Census Dashboard**, which will then redirect you to the detailed dashboard view. In the detailed dashboard view, you will see all visuals that are part of that dashboard. You can click on the arrow to the extreme top right of each visual to open the specific chart in full screen mode, as shown in the following screenshot. In the scatter plot analysis shown here, you can further click on any of the dots to get specific values about that bubble.

The selected circle is for zip code **94027**, which has a **PopulationCount** of **7,089** and **MedianIncome** of **$216,905.00** and **MeanIncome** of **336,888**:

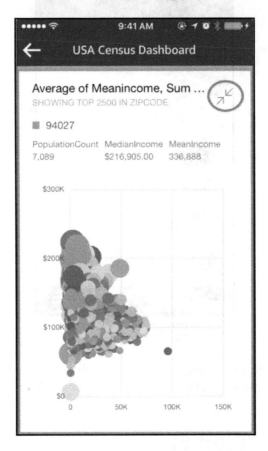

Figure 6.3: Dashboard visual

One caution: while the detailed view allows you to focus on a bubble in the chart, it does not support zoom in like a standard image viewing application would behave.

Find your dashboard

The QuickSight mobile app also provides a search feature, which is particularly useful when you have several dashboards and only know a partial name. Here are the steps to search for a dashboard:

1. First ensure you are in the **Dashboards** tab by clicking on the **Dashboards** icon from the bottom menu.
2. Next, click on the search icon seen in the top-right corner.
3. Next, type the partial name. In the following example, I have typed Usa.
4. QuickSight now searches for all dashboards that have the word Usa in them and lists them out.
5. You can now click on the dashboard to get the details about that specific dashboard, as shown in the following screenshot:

Figure 6.4: Dashboard search

QuickSight search is limited to just the dashboard name; it does not search for any other attributes like field names or the dataset itself.

Favorite a dashboard

QuickSight provides a convenient way to access your favorite dashboards. To use this feature, first identify which dashboards you use often and click on the star icon to its right-hand side, as shown in the following screenshot. Next, to access all of your favorites, click on the **Favorites** tab and the list is then refined to only those dashboards that you had previously identified as favorites:

Figure 6.5: Dashboard favorites

Limitations of the mobile app

While dashboards are fairly easy to interact with on the mobile app, there are key limitations when compared to the standard browser version, which I am listing as follows:

- The app currently supports only Apple devices
- You cannot create or share dashboards to others using the mobile app
- You cannot zoom in/out from the visual, which would be really good in scenarios where the charts are dense
- Chart legends are not shown
- The search feature is very basic and only supports names

Most of these features are being addressed in the next releases of the product.

Analyses on the go

To access your saved analyses, click on the **Analyses** icon from the menu at the bottom of your mobile device; you will then see a list of analyses, as shown in this screenshot:

Figure 6.6: Analysis list

In the next few sections, we will review how to navigate other analysis features.

View details of your analysis

From the listing of analyses, select the **AWS Usage Metrics** analysis, which will then redirect you to the detailed analysis view. In the detailed view, you will see all visuals that are part of that analysis. You can click on the arrow to the extreme top right of each visual to open the specific chart in full screen mode. The visuals also come with the date slider to change the date range shown in the chart. To change the chart type for the visual, click on the bar-like icon on the bottom left, as shown in the following screenshot:

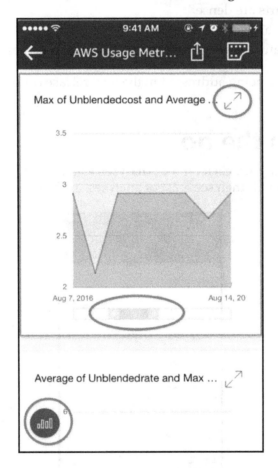

Figure 6.7: Analysis details

For the area line chart shown in the preceding screenshot, after you click to change the visuals type, you will get a popup in the bottom with all the chart types. From the list, select the line chart as shown in the following screenshot to see the chart type change:

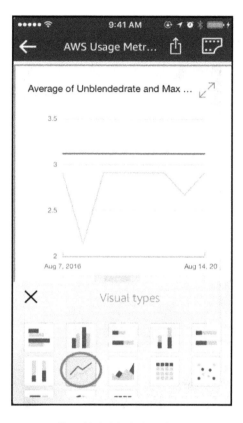

Figure 6.8: Analysis visual type change

Share your analysis

With the mobile app, you can share your analysis with your peers using the share button in the top-right corner:

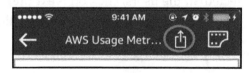

Figure 6.9: Analysis sharing

After you click on the share option, QuickSight will redirect you to the **Invite User** page, where you can enable sharing with existing users, as shown in the following screenshot:

Figure 6.10: Analysis sharing add users

I will now detail the steps for inviting users:

1. If you see the user you want to grant access to, click on the check mark till it converts to a green sign.
2. If you do not see the user, you can search users by name or e-mail address.
3. Once you have selected all the users, click on **Next Step**.
4. You will then be redirected to a confirmation screen; click on **Confirm and Share**.

This makes sharing analysis really easy using your mobile device.

Stories related to analysis

With the mobile app, you can view stories related to your analysis using the stories button on the top-right corner, as shown in the following screenshot:

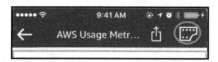

Figure 6.11: Analysis stories

 This stories icon will be enabled only if there are stories related to the analysis.

Search for analysis

Search for analysis works similarly to search for dashboards. Follow these steps to search for an analysis:

1. First ensure you are in the **Analyses** tab by clicking on the **Analyses** icon from the bottom menu.
2. Next click on the search icon seen in the top-right corner.
3. Next type the partial name. In the following example, I have typed `Aws`.
4. QuickSight now searches for all analyses that have the word `Aws` in them and lists them out.

5. You can now click on the analysis to get details about that specific analysis, as shown in this screenshot:

Figure 6.12: Analysis search

Favorite your analysis

Similar to dashboards, you can also favorite your analysis for ease of access. To use this feature, first identify which analysis you use often and click on the star icon to its right. Next, to access all of your favorites, click on the **Favorites** tab and the list is then refined to only those analysis you had previously identified as favorites, as shown in the following screenshot:

Figure 6.13: Analysis favorites

Limitations of the mobile app

The following are the key limitations compared to the standard browser version:

- You cannot create a new analysis using the mobile app
- While you can temporarily change the visual type for existing charts in an analysis, you cannot change the fields nor can you add new visuals to the analysis
- You cannot zoom in/out from the visual, which would be really good in scenarios where the charts are dense
- Chart legends are not shown

Stories on the go

To access your saved analyses, click on **Stories** icon from the menu at the bottom of your mobile device; you will then see a list of stories, as shown in the following screenshot:

Figure 6.14: Story listing

In the next few sections we will review how to navigate other features related to stories.

Story detailed view

From the stories listing, select **USA Census StoryBoard**, which will then redirect you to the detailed view for that story. In the detailed view, you will see all visuals that are part of that story, as shown in the following screenshot:

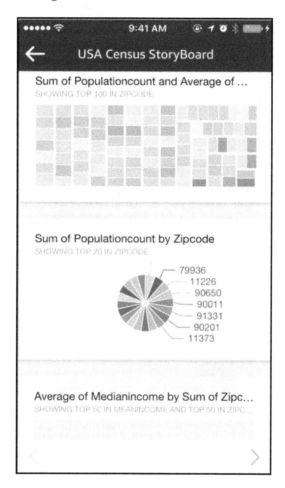

Figure 6.15: Story details

Search your stories

Story search works similarly to search for dashboards. Follow these steps to search for a story:

1. First ensure you are in the **Stories** tab by clicking on the **Stories** icon from the bottom menu.
2. Next click on the search icon seen in the top-right corner.
3. Next type the partial name. In the following example, I have typed `Salary`.
4. QuickSight now searches for all stories that have the word `Salary` in them and lists them out.
5. You can click on the story to get the details of that specific story, as shown in the following screenshot:

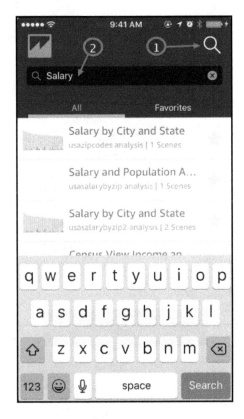

Figure 6.16: Story search

Favorite a story

Similar to dashboards, you can favorite a story. To use this feature, first identify which story you often use and click on the star icon to its right. Next, to access all of your favorites, click on the **Favorites** tab and the list is then refined to only those stories you had previously identified as favorite.

Advanced options for the QuickSight mobile app

Let's review the configurations provided in the QuickSight app. To get to these configurations, click on the **More** icon from the bottom menu, as shown in the following screenshot:

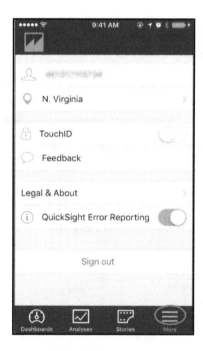

Figure 6.17: Advanced options

I'll highlight the key aspects of the advanced configuration as follows:

- By default, QuickSight will display data from the **N. Virginia** region, which corresponds to us-east-1 region. If your QuickSight account is in one of the other regions (us-west-1 or eu-west-1), you can switch it by clicking on the > next to the word **N. Virginia**.
- If you wish to use the Apple **TouchID** for authentication, turn on the **TouchID** option, as shown in the preceding screenshot.
- The QuickSight development team can be easily contacted with the **Feedback** option, which drafts and e-mails the support team.
- You can turn off **QuickSight Error Reporting** if you desire; by default, it is turned on.

Summary

The QuickSight iOS app complements the standard browser-based application and provides BI on the go. You can stay connected to your data from anywhere, anytime on your iPhone, iPad, and iPod touch. Using this app, you can browse, search, and view dashboards, analyses, and stories from a simple menu at the bottom of the application. QuickSight allows you to favorite commonly used items so that you can quickly access them next time. Additionally, it allows you to share analysis with your peers.

All interactions on mobile devices are read-only and do not get persisted on QuickSight servers so that one does not accidentally change things while demonstrating using the mobile device. The mobile app does have some limitations, notably the lack of creating new or editing existing analyses and no option to zoom in/out for dense visuals.

Finally, a reminder: the mobile app is certified only for iOS devices and the Android application is coming soon.

7
Big Data Analytics Mini Project

Modern data architectures are moving to a data lake solution that has the ability to ingest data from various sources, transform and analyze at a big data scale. In the last few chapters, we saw various AWS components that help in big data analytics; Amazon now offers a data lake solution that packages the most commonly needed components along with a web application to jump-start the data lake build-out. In this chapter, we will solve a real-life use case leveraging the AWS Data Lake solution and we will cover the following topics:

- Overview of AWS Data Lake solution
- AWS Data Lake architecture
- A Mini project on AWS Data Lake
- Advanced AWS Data Lake features

Overview of AWS Data Lake solution

A **data lake** is a new architectural pattern that is a popular way to store and analyze data as it allows enterprises to easily ingest and store data in any format, both structured and unstructured. A modern data lake provides more agility and flexibility than traditional management systems and allows businesses to store all their data, structured and unstructured, in a central repository.

In Chapter 2, *Exploring Any Data*, we looked at various services that make up an AWS big data ecosystem. These services are building blocks for a data lake and are broadly classified into four major categories: collect, store, analyze, and orchestrate.

To jump start the build-out of a new data lake, AWS offers a data lake solution that has the key building blocks already packaged and deployed, along with an intuitive web application. This pre-packaged implementation allows customers to quickly realize the data lake concept and put a real web interface in front of the data lake to register new data feeds with metadata, catalog, search, and provisioning. The following are the key features provided by the AWS Data Lake solution:

- **Reference implementation**: In AWS Data Lake solution, you are provided with an out-of-the-box implementation, including metadata management, that you can customize as per your project needs.
- **User interface**: The solution comes packaged with a web-based user interface hosted on S3. Use this to manage data lake users, policies, and packages. You can also use it to search for data packages and create manifests for provisioning it to target databases.
- **APIs**: AWS Data Lake solution comes with APIs or CLI to automate integration with other services in AWS and help in onboarding or extracting data to and from the data lake. The solution also comes with API key management by user.
- **Central storage layer**: For data lake storage, use the S3 bucket and secure it with AWS key management service to encrypt data at rest.

Data lake core concept – package

Before we get further into the AWS Data Lake solution, we must be familiar with a core concept called **package**. It is basically a logical concept that groups all files that have the same structure into one unit called a package. Let's take an example: say you are receiving user web clicks information daily as a file from your web application, as a TSV file stored in S3 under a folder. To use this dataset in the AWS Data Lake, you will first have to create a package with a name like *user web clicks* and define the structure (fields with data types) and the location of the files.

AWS Data Lake architecture

Let's look at the data lake architecture with AWS Data Lake solution. The overall services provided by a data lake can be grouped into the following four categories:

- Managed ingestion to onboard data from various sources and any format
- Centralized storage that can scale as per the business needs

- Processing and analyzing at big data scale in various programming languages
- Governing and securing your data packages

The next diagram shows the overall architecture that will form a data lake in AWS. Let's review each feature category in detail:

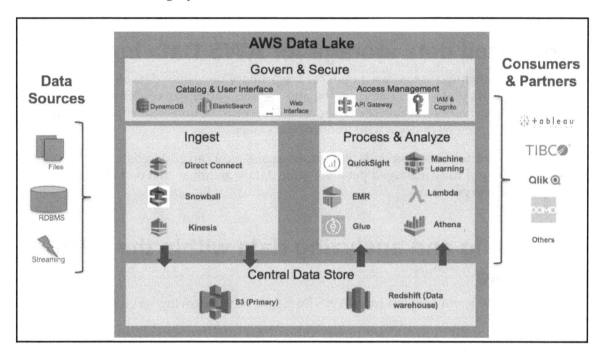

Figure 7.1: AWS data lake architecture

Managed data ingestion to AWS Data Lake

Amazon has several tools that can ingest data to S3 and Redshift, and I will discuss the most common options here: Direct Connect, Snowball, and Kinesis. Let's review each of these options at a high level:

- **Direct Connect**: With Direct Connect, you can establish private connectivity between AWS and your enterprise data center and provide an easy way to move data files from your applications to the AWS S3 storage layer of your data lake

- **Snowball**: Snowball (also known as import/export) lets you import hundreds of terabytes of data quickly into AWS using Amazon-provided secure appliances for secure transport
- **Kinesis and Kinesis Firehose**: Kinesis services enable the building of custom applications that process or analyze streaming data

Centralized data storage for AWS Data Lake

AWS Data Lake architecture is based on S3 as the primary persistent data store for your cluster. This allows you to separate compute and storage, and resize on demand with no data loss. It is also highly durable and low-cost with several options to connect. We can share data by sharing S3 buckets with multiple data lakes.

Optionally, if your use case demands SQL-based access, you can add Redshift to the storage layer. It is a fast and fully managed petabyte-scale data warehouse that costs less than $1,000 per terabyte per year.

Processing and analyzing data within the AWS Data Lake

For data processing and analysis in an AWS Data Lake, the following services are available:

- **QuickSight**: A fast, cloud-powered **business intelligence** (**BI**) service and the theme of this book.
- **Machine learning**: Machine learning provides visualization tools and wizards for creating machine learning models and executing them on your big data.
- **EMR:** Amazon EMR provides a distributed compute framework that makes it an easy, fast, and cost-effective way to process data on S3 at scale and on demand. AWS now provides options for spot instances that are offered at lower cost. They are best used for application tests and/or use cases that don't have hard SLA's.
- **Lambda**: AWS Lambda allows you to run code without provisioning or managing the server and can be triggered upon arrival of data in S3 and for any streaming sources from Kinesis.
- **Athena**: A query service that makes it easy to analyze data directly from files in S3 using standard SQL statements. Athena is server-less, which makes it really stand out since there is no additional infrastructure to be provisioned.

- **Glue**: A new service that enables ETL and makes it easy to transform and move data from S3 to your consumers. It is integrated with S3, Redshift, and other JDBC complaint data sources and auto-suggests schemas and transformations, which improve developer productivity. You can also view and edit the code it generates in popular languages such as Python and Spark, with the ability to share the code with your peers. Glue schedules the ETL jobs and auto-provisions and scales the infrastructure based on the job requirements.

Governing and securing the AWS Data Lake

Governance is key in building a managed data lake and this area is where the AWS solution has made recent efforts by introducing catalog and a web interface. Let's review the key services used for governance:

- **Catalog and user interface**: AWS Data Lake solution comes with a data catalog that is searchable using the web application. The catalog can be populated by the web interface or via the API with information about the various packages for the data lake, and this information is stored in DynamoDB. Once the datasets are registered, they are automatically indexed to Elasticsearch and are searchable by the web interface.
- **User and access management**: AWS Data Lake solution provides a web interface to manage users for the data lake. As a data lake administrator, you can decide which user gets access to the data lake and at what level (member or administrator). You can also grant API access to specific users.

This concludes the AWS Data Lake architecture; next, we will build a real-life use case using AWS Data Lake.

A mini project on AWS Data Lake

In this section, we will build a completely new data lake using the AWS Data Lake solution. We will first review the business use case; then we will build the cluster, ingest data, and process the data; finally, we will analyze it using QuickSight.

Mini use case business context

For this mini use case, we are going to analyze air quality data from various states in the USA and see whether there is any relationship between population trends and air quality over time. Let's review the source datasets for this project.

Air quality index

The **Environmental Protection Agency** (**EPA**) calculates the air quality index based on the concentration of pollutants. The following are the key measures tracked to determine air quality:

- Ozone (O_3)
- Carbon monoxide (CO)
- Sulfur dioxide (SO_2)
- Nitrogen dioxide (NO_2)
- Inhalable particulates (PM_{10})
- Fine particulates ($PM_{2.5}$)
- Lead (Pb)

To make analysis easier, EPA tracks the number of days in a year with good air quality for every major city in USA and this is tracked every year. For further details about the EPA air quality report, visit this site: `https://www.epa.gov/outdoor-air-quality-data/about-air-data-reports#con`

Census population

The US Census Bureau Population Estimates Program produces estimates for its cities, counties, and states by year. This information is available in the US Census Bureau website here: `http://www.census.gov/programs-surveys/popest.html`

Deploying AWS Data Lake using CloudFormation

AWS Data Lake solution is based on CloudFormation (`https://aws.amazon.com/cloudformation/`).

Follow the next steps to deploy a new data lake solution in your account.

Creating a new stack

Here are the steps to launch a new stack:

1. Log in to the AWS management console and select **CloudFormation** under the management services as shown here:

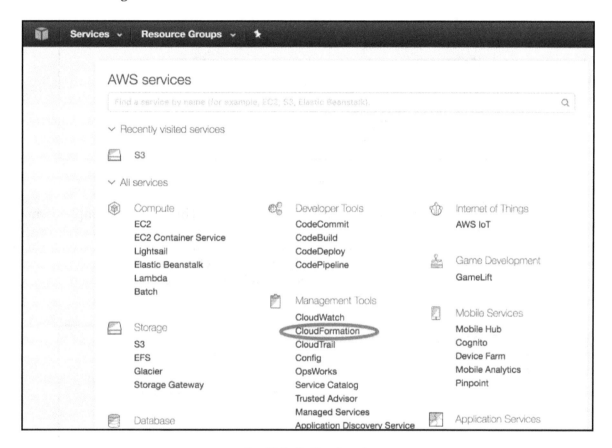

Figure 7.2: The CloudFormation service

2. Next, click on **Create New Stack** as shown in the following screenshot:

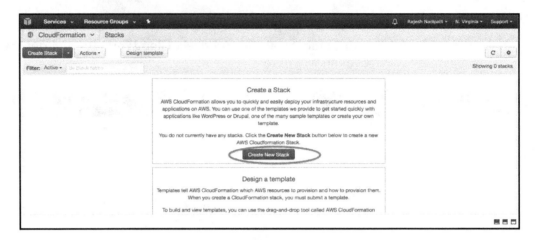

Figure 7.3: Create new stack

3. Select the option to upload a template to Amazon S3. This data lake template can be found at `https://s3.amazonaws.com/solutions-reference/data-lake-sol ution/latest/data-lake-deploy.template`, and also on my GitHub account at `https://github.com/rnadipalli/quicksight/blob/master/miniproject/con fig/data-lake-deploy.template`. See the following screenshot to understand this:

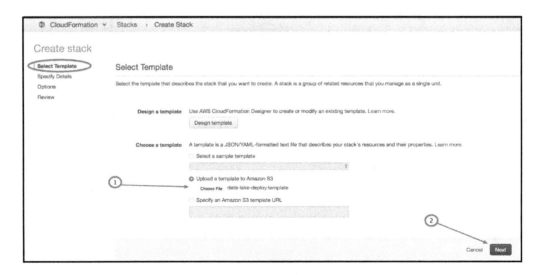

Figure 7.4: Upload data lake template

4. Next, you will see the stack details screen, where you need to enter the mandatory information explained here:
    - **Stack name**: You can set this as `PolutionAnalysisDL` for the pollution analysis data lake
    - **Administrator name**: This is the user ID that will be the main administrator for the data lake
    - **Administrator email address**: Enter a valid e-mail address associated with the administrator user
    - **Administrator Access IP for Elasticsearch cluster**: Enter the IP address range from where the administrator(s) will access the necessary management function, for example, `106.10.172.0/0`
    - **Send Anonymous Usage Data**: Select **No** if you want to opt out from sending usage information to AWS
5. Once done, click on the **Next** button to move to the next screen. See the following screenshot with these options:

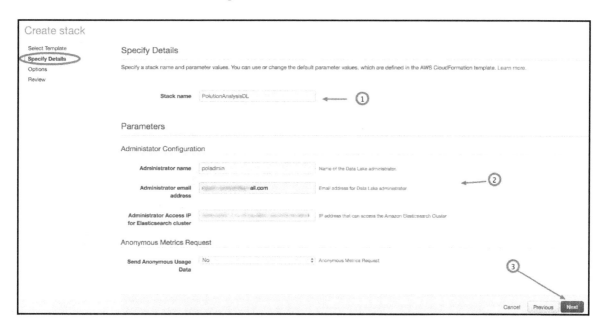

Figure 7.5: Create stack detailed options

6. You will see the **Options** page, where you can specify optional tags (key-value pairs) for your stack. In this case, we will skip and click on **Next** to continue.

7. Now you will see the final **Review** page, where you can confirm the settings. Ensure that you check the **I acknowledge...** checkbox and then click on **Create** to start the creation process:

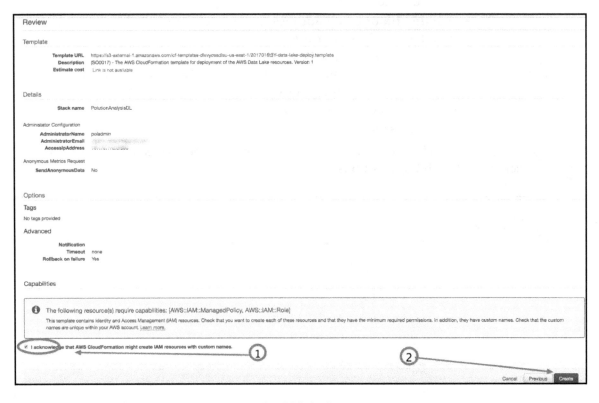

Figure 7.6: Stack review

This completes the setup and now AWS will launch four stacks for the data lake solution. You will see the following screen after successful creation, which takes about 25 minutes:

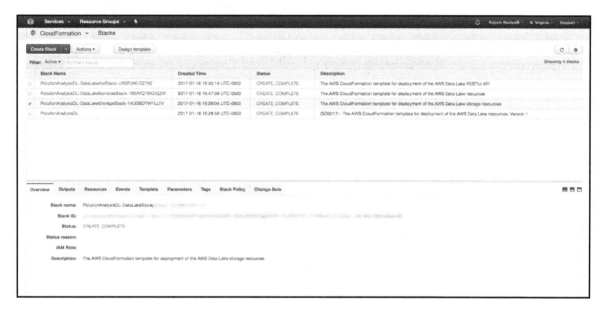

Figure 7.7: Stack creation confirmation

This completes the deployment of the data lake; next, we will review how to access this.

Access your data lake stack

Here are the steps required to access your newly created data lake:

1. After the data lake is created, the administrator will receive an e-mail that contains the URL to get to the data lake console and a temporary password.
2. Click on the URL and you will be prompted to change the password.

3. You can also click on the stack listing page and then on the link for `PolutionAnalysisDL`. It will take you to the stack details page for this, as shown in the following screenshot, which also provides the URL for the data lake console:

Figure 7.8: DL stack details

4. Next, open the data lake console in a new tab and you will see the following login page:

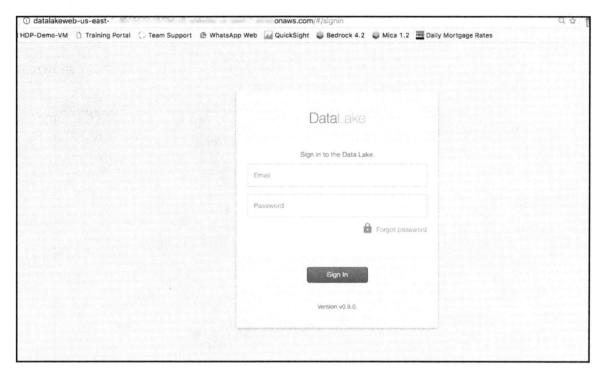

Figure 7.9: Data lake console login

This completes the data lake access section; next, we will review the data sources and ingest them into the data lake.

Acquiring the data for the mini project

For this mini project, I have downloaded data from some public websites and saved it on GitHub at this location: `https://github.com/rnadipalli/quicksight/tree/master/mini project/datasets`.

For EPA air quality data, I have seven files, one for each year from 2010 to 2016, as shown in this screenshot:

Figure 7.10: EPA Air Quality Index (AQI) datasets

For the USA population data, I have consolidated it as a single file as shown here:

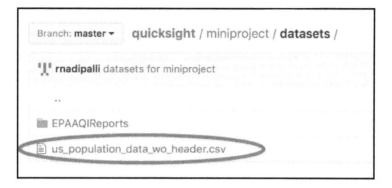

Figure 7.11: US population estimates

Hydrating the data lake

Now that we have acquired the source data, we will review the steps to hydrate the data lake with these datasets. The AWS Data Lake architecture recommends that all source data should be ingested into S3 buckets. In this section, we will discuss the steps needed to ingest data to an S3 bucket created for this project: `quicksight-mini-project`.

Air quality index data in S3

Here are the steps to load EPA data to S3:

1. First download the data file from GitHub (`https://github.com/rnadipalli/quicksight/tree/master/miniproject/datasets/EPAAQIReports`) to your local desktop.
2. Create a folder under the S3 bucket and name it `EPAaqidata`. Create seven subfolders under it, one for each year, such as `year=2010`.
3. Upload the data files to the respective year folder.

4. Finally, your folder structure should look like this:

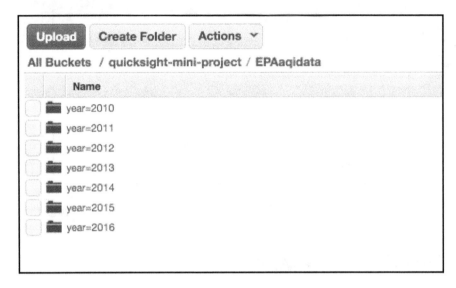

Figure 7.12: EPA AQI data in S3

US population data in S3

Here are the steps to load the US population estimates data into S3:

1. First, download the data file from GitHub (https://github.com/rnadipalli/qu icksight/blob/master/miniproject/datasets/us_population_data_wo_head er.csv) to your local desktop.

2. Next, create a folder under the S3 bucket and name it Populationdata.

3. Upload the data file under the S3 bucket location quicksight-mini-project/Populationdata folder.

This completes the hydration (data ingestion) to the AWS Data Lake; next, we will review how to catalog the datasets.

Cataloging data assets

In this section, we will review how to leverage the AWS Data Lake packaged metadata management web interface to categorize, tag, and catalog data assets.

Creating governance tags

As we onboard data to the data lake, it is important to record the business context of the data so that consumers can easily identify the data. AWS Data Lake solution makes it really easy for data stewards to specify these tags as and when datasets are registered to the data lake. For our mini project, we follow these steps to create these governance tags:

1. First, log in to the data lake console with the administration credentials.
2. From the navigation pane on the left, choose **Settings** under the **Administration** section.
3. Next, click on the **Governance** tab and select **Add Tag Governance**.
4. Enter the following tag names:
   - `Retention Years` to track the retention period of the dataset
   - `Category` to track the category of the dataset `EPA` or `Census`
   - `Data Steward` to track the username of the data steward
   - `PII Indicator` to track if there is any **Personal Identifiable Information** (**PII**) in the datasets
5. Click on **Save** to update the data lake governance settings.

This completes the governance settings as shown in the following screenshot:

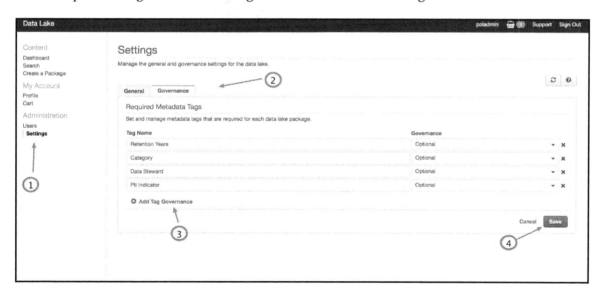

Figure 7.13: Governance tag setup

Registering data packages

In this section, we will review how to register the two data packages for this mini project with AWS Data Lake solution.

EPA AQI data package

Let's see the steps required to create the EPA AQI data package:

1. First, log in to the data lake console with the administration credentials.
2. From the navigation pane on the left, choose **Create a Package** under the **Content** section.
3. Next, enter the package name, description, and governance tags.
4. Click on the **Create package** button and this creates the new package.
5. The following screenshot shows the **Create a Package** screen for the EPA dataset:

Figure 7.14: EPA AQI package registration basic tab

Next, follow these steps to add content to the newly created package:

1. Click on the **Content** tab of the EPA AQI package.
2. Create a manifest file that has a list of all S3 files for EPA AQI data, as follows:

```
{
  "fileLocations": [
    {
      "url": "s3://quicksight-mini-
         project/EPAaqidata/year=2010/aqireport2010.csv"
    },
    {
      "url": "s3://quicksight-mini-
         project/EPAaqidata/year=2011/aqireport2011.csv"
    },
    {
      "url": "s3://quicksight-mini-
         project/EPAaqidata/year=2012/aqireport2012.csv"
    },
    {
      "url": "s3://quicksight-mini-
         project/EPAaqidata/year=2013/aqireport2013.csv"
    },
    {
      "url": "s3://quicksight-mini-
         project/EPAaqidata/year=2014/aqireport2014.csv"
    },
    {
      "url": "s3://quicksight-mini-
         project/EPAaqidata/year=2015/aqireport2015.csv"
    },
    {
      "url": "s3://quicksight-mini-
         project/EPAaqidata/year=2016/aqireport2016.csv"
    }
  ]
}
```

3. Upload the manifest file just created to the content. For your convenience, I have uploaded this file on GitHub at `https://github.com/rnadipalli/quicksight /blob/master/miniproject/config/EPAAQIManifest.json`.

4. Next, click on **Save** as shown in the following screenshot:

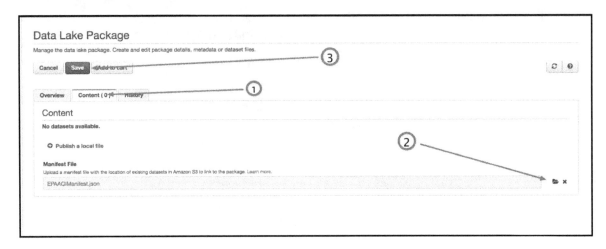

Figure 7.15: EPA AQI S3 manifest file upload

After successfully linking the S3 files to the package, you will see the following screen, with a list of all seven files imported from the S3 manifest file:

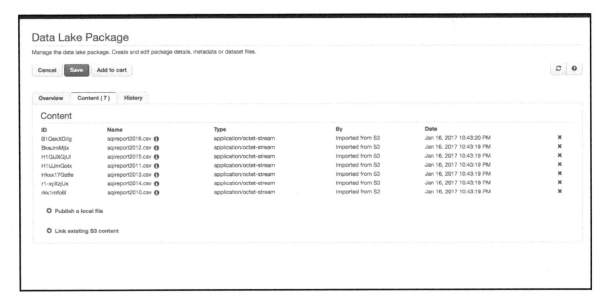

Figure 7.16: PA AQI data content review

You can optionally review the **History** tab of the package to see all activity for that package, as shown here:

Figure 7.17: Package history

This completes the registration of the EPA AQI package to AWS Data Lake.

USA population history package

Similar to the EPA AQI package, you can create the USA population history package. I will highlight the key steps for this package:

1. From the navigation pane on the left, choose **Create a Package** under the **Content** section.

2. Next, enter the package name, description, and governance tags as shown in the following screenshot:

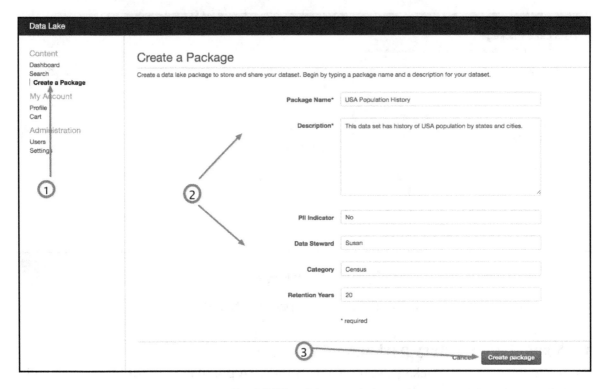

Figure 7.18: USA population create package

3. Next, link the S3 files to the package using the following manifest file: `https://g ithub.com/rnadipalli/quicksight/blob/master/miniproject/config/Popul ationHistoryManifest.json`.

4. Click on **Save** to complete registration.

This completes the registration of the USA population package to AWS Data Lake.

Searching the data catalog

Once the data packages are registered to the data lake, the AWS solution automatically indexes this data and provides a very easy-to-use search interface. This enables data consumers to search packages available in the data lake based on their interest. Let's review the key steps to use search:

1. First log in to the data lake console.
2. From the navigation pane on the left, choose **Search** under the **Content** section.
3. Enter the search term in the provided textbox. You can use * as wild character if needed.
4. Click on the **Search** button to submit your query and see the results, as shown in the following screenshot:

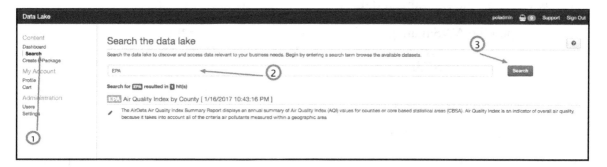

Figure 7.19: Search catalog

From the results list, you can click on the **Edit** icon to go straight to the package and edit if needed. This completes the data package registration and search section.

Extracting packages using manifest

Once you've found some data that you like, you can add it to the cart and generate manifest files with secure access links to the desired content. Let's review the steps for this:

1. From the search results, first select the packages that you want to extract to your cart such as a shopping experience.
2. Next, click on the **Cart** icon from the **Cart** menu on the left navigation menu.
3. To check out your items, click on the **My Cart** icon seen on the top right.
4. Finally, click on **Generate Manifest** to generate the manifest file.

One example of using this manifest metadata is to export data from S3 to Redshift database using a script leveraging the manifest file. Next, let's look at how to process data in a data lake.

Processing data in the AWS Data Lake

In this section, we will review how to prepare the data that is now registered with the data lake and get some insights from it.

Creating Athena tables

There are several options to process the data; for this mini project, we will leverage Athena to create tables on the centralized data store S3, using the following steps:

1. Open the AWS management console for Athena using this link: `https://consol e.aws.amazon.com/athena/home`. Alternatively, search for Athena in the AWS services search bar.

2. Using the Query Editor, run the create database statement as shown in the next screenshot with the query:

   ```
   CREATE DATABASE polutionanalysisdb;
   ```

3. Next, create a new table for the EPA AQI package in S3 with a partition clause:

   ```
   CREATE EXTERNAL TABLE IF NOT EXISTS
     polutionanalysisdb.epaaqi_raw (
     `City_Code` int,
     `City_Name` string,
     `Days_with_AQI` int,
     `Good_Days` int,
     `Moderate_Days` int,
     `Unhealthy_for_Sensitive_Days` int,
     `Unhealthy_Days` int,
     `Very_Unhealthy_Days` int,
     `AQI_Maximum` int,
     `AQI_90th_Percentile` int,
     `AQI_Median` int,
     `CO_Days` int,
     `NO2_Days` int,
     `O3_Days` int,
     `SO2_Days` int,
     `PM25_Days` int,
     `PM10_Days` int
   ```

```
)
PARTITIONED BY (year string)
ROW FORMAT SERDE
  'org.apache.hadoop.hive.serde2.lazy.LazySimpleSerDe'
WITH SERDEPROPERTIES (
  'serialization.format' = ',',
  'field.delim' = '|'
) LOCATION 's3://quicksight-mini-project/EPAaqidata/';
```

4. The preceding query is on GitHub, at `https://github.com/rnadipalli/quicksight/blob/master/miniproject/sqlscripts/athenaddl.sql`.

5. Next, to load all partitions of the table, run the following command:

```
MSCK REPAIR TABLE polutionanalysisdb.epaaqi_raw;
```

6. You can now query the table and view data as shown here:

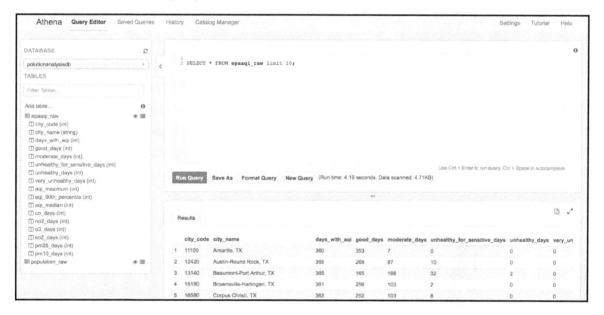

Figure 7.20: EPA AQI report query

7. Next, create a new table for the history of USA population using the following SQL statement, which is also present on GitHub at `https://github.com/rnadipalli/quicksight/blob/master/miniproject/sqlscripts/athenaddl.sql`:

```
CREATE EXTERNAL TABLE IF NOT EXISTS
  polutionanalysisdb.population_raw (
```

```
SUMLEV int,
REGION int,
DIVISION int,
STATE string,
COUNTY string,
STNAME string,
CTYNAME string,
CENSUS2010POP int,
ESTIMATESBASE2010 int,
POPESTIMATE2010 int,
POPESTIMATE2011 int,
POPESTIMATE2012 int,
POPESTIMATE2013 int,
POPESTIMATE2014 int,
POPESTIMATE2015 int,
NPOPCHG_2010 int,
NPOPCHG_2011 int,
NPOPCHG_2012 int,
NPOPCHG_2013 int,
NPOPCHG_2014 int,
NPOPCHG_2015 int,
BIRTHS2010 int,
BIRTHS2011 int,
BIRTHS2012 int,
BIRTHS2013 int,
BIRTHS2014 int,
BIRTHS2015 int,
DEATHS2010 int,
DEATHS2011 int,
DEATHS2012 int,
DEATHS2013 int,
DEATHS2014 int,
DEATHS2015 int,
NATURALINC2010 int,
NATURALINC2011 int,
NATURALINC2012 int,
NATURALINC2013 int,
NATURALINC2014 int,
NATURALINC2015 int,
INTERNATIONALMIG2010 int,
INTERNATIONALMIG2011 int,
INTERNATIONALMIG2012 int,
INTERNATIONALMIG2013 int,
INTERNATIONALMIG2014 int,
INTERNATIONALMIG2015 int,
DOMESTICMIG2010 int,
DOMESTICMIG2011 int,
DOMESTICMIG2012 int,
```

```
DOMESTICMIG2013 int,
DOMESTICMIG2014 int,
DOMESTICMIG2015 int,
NETMIG2010 int,
NETMIG2011 int,
NETMIG2012 int,
NETMIG2013 int,
NETMIG2014 int,
NETMIG2015 int,
RESIDUAL2010 int,
RESIDUAL2011 int,
RESIDUAL2012 int,
RESIDUAL2013 int,
RESIDUAL2014 int,
RESIDUAL2015 int,
GQESTIMATESBASE2010 int,
GQESTIMATES2010 int,
GQESTIMATES2011 int,
GQESTIMATES2012 int,
GQESTIMATES2013 int,
GQESTIMATES2014 int,
GQESTIMATES2015 int,
RBIRTH2011 float,
RBIRTH2012 float,
RBIRTH2013 float,
RBIRTH2014 float,
RBIRTH2015 float,
RDEATH2011 float,
RDEATH2012 float,
RDEATH2013 float,
RDEATH2014 float,
RDEATH2015 float,
RNATURALINC2011 float,
RNATURALINC2012 float,
RNATURALINC2013 float,
RNATURALINC2014 float,
RNATURALINC2015 float,
RINTERNATIONALMIG2011 float,
RINTERNATIONALMIG2012 float,
RINTERNATIONALMIG2013 float,
RINTERNATIONALMIG2014 float,
RINTERNATIONALMIG2015 float,
RDOMESTICMIG2011 float,
RDOMESTICMIG2012 float,
RDOMESTICMIG2013 float,
RDOMESTICMIG2014 float,
RDOMESTICMIG2015 float,
RNETMIG2011 float,
```

```
   RNETMIG2012 float,
   RNETMIG2013 float,
   RNETMIG2014 float,
   RNETMIG2015 float
)
ROW FORMAT SERDE
   'org.apache.hadoop.hive.serde2.lazy.LazySimpleSerDe'
WITH SERDEPROPERTIES (
   'serialization.format' = ',', 'field.delim' = ',' )
LOCATION 's3://quicksight-mini-project/Populationdata/';
```

8. Verify that the table is working by running a simple Select statement on the new table.

This completes the registration of tables in Athena; next, we will see how to analyze this data using QuickSight.

Analyzing using QuickSight

As they say, the best comes last. To finally make sense of the data and build interesting reports, we will use QuickSight for this mini project.

Population analysis

In this section, we will build reports to understand the impact of population on air quality over time. First, we will analyze and report the population trend and then overlay the EPA air quality data to see if there is a relationship between the data.

Creating the population dataset

Follow these steps to create a new dataset for population analysis:

1. From the **Manage data**, create a new dataset of type Athena and set the name as `population_raw`. Enter the data source name as `polutionanalysisdb`, the same as the Athena database name.

2. The raw dataset is a flat structure with one row per city/state and different columns for population estimates for each year. With the custom SQL option, we will transform this data into multiple rows for easier reporting.

3. In the **Data source** section, select the **Query** option and enter the following custom SQL:

```
select stname, county, ctyname, '2010' as year,
    census2010pop as populationcount
from polutionanalysisdb.population_raw
where county != '0'
union
select stname, county, ctyname, '2011' as year,
    popestimate2011 as populationcount
from polutionanalysisdb.population_raw
where county != '0'
union
select stname, county, ctyname, '2012' as year,
    popestimate2012 as populationcount
from polutionanalysisdb.population_raw
where county != '0'
union
select stname, county, ctyname, '2013' as year,
    popestimate2013 as populationcount
from polutionanalysisdb.population_raw
where county != '0'
union
select stname, county, ctyname, '2014' as year,
    popestimate2014 as populationcount
from polutionanalysisdb.population_raw
where county != '0'
union
select stname, county, ctyname, '2015' as year,
    popestimate2015 as populationcount
from polutionanalysisdb.population_raw
where county != '0'
```

4. It should now show you results like this:

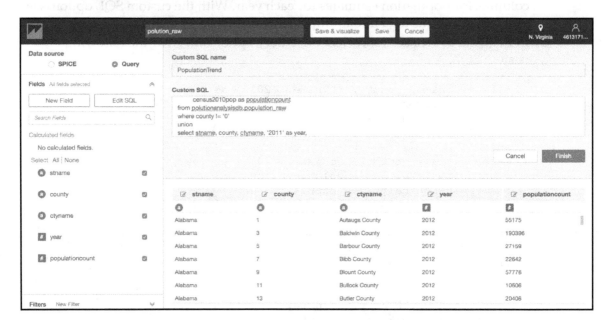

Figure 7.21: Dataset for population

5. Click on **Finish** to save this new dataset.
6. Now your dataset is ready for analysis.

Insights from population dataset

In this section, we will visualize data from population data. Follow these steps to create charts:

1. Create a new analysis using the `population_raw` dataset created in the previous section.
2. Next, we will create a bar chart to see the population count by state for the year 2015. For this, we will select the **Visual type** as **Vertical stacked bar chart** and then select **stname** as **X axis**, **Populationcount (sum)** as **Y axis**, and year for **Group/Color**.

3. Next, we filter the year to **2015** so that we get the latest population estimates, as shown in this screenshot:

Figure 7.22: Population bar chart

4. This shows that California is the most populous state, followed by Texas.

5. Next, let's see the trend of population over time using a line chart, as shown here:

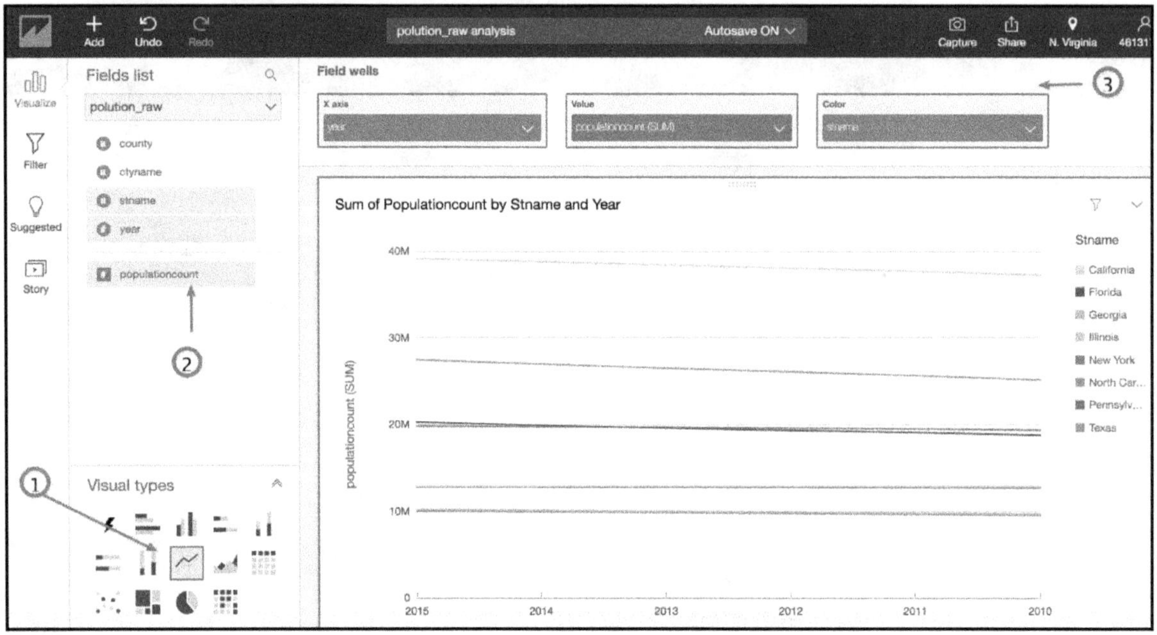

Figure 7.23: Population trend

This completes our insights on population. Next, let's see if the population has any impact on the air quality index.

Combining population and EPA datasets

To complete our initial quest, we need to combine the population data and the EPA AQI data using the following steps:

1. From the **Manage data**, create a new dataset of type Athena and set the name as `epaaqi_raw`. Enter data source name as `polutionanalysisdb2`.

2. For this analysis, we will select the city of Austin, Texas, and see how the population increase has impacted the air quality.

3. For this, we will join the two datasets using the following SQL statement, which is also available on GitHub at `https://github.com/rnadipalli/quicksight/blob/master/miniproject/sqlscripts/QuickSight-custom-queries.sql`:

```
select polr.year, popr.ctyname, popr.census2010pop as
```

```
      PopulationCount ,
      polr.Good_Days, polr.Moderate_Days,
        polr.Unhealthy_for_Sensitive_Days, polr.Unhealthy_Days,
          polr.Very_Unhealthy_Days
from polutionanalysisdb.population_raw popr,
   polutionanalysisdb.epaaqi_raw polr
where popr.stname = 'Texas'
and    popr.ctyname like 'Austin%'
and    polr.city_name LIKE 'Austin%'
and    polr.year = '2010'
UNION
select polr.year, popr.ctyname, popr.POPESTIMATE2011 as
   PopulationCount ,
      polr.Good_Days, polr.Moderate_Days,
        polr.Unhealthy_for_Sensitive_Days, polr.Unhealthy_Days,
          polr.Very_Unhealthy_Days
from polutionanalysisdb.population_raw popr,
   polutionanalysisdb.epaaqi_raw polr
where popr.stname = 'Texas'
and    popr.ctyname like 'Austin%'
and    polr.city_name LIKE 'Austin%'
and    polr.year = '2011'
UNION
select polr.year, popr.ctyname, popr.POPESTIMATE2012 as
   PopulationCount ,
      polr.Good_Days, polr.Moderate_Days,
        polr.Unhealthy_for_Sensitive_Days, polr.Unhealthy_Days,
          polr.Very_Unhealthy_Days
from polutionanalysisdb.population_raw popr,
   polutionanalysisdb.epaaqi_raw polr
where popr.stname = 'Texas'
and    popr.ctyname like 'Austin%'
and    polr.city_name LIKE 'Austin%'
and    polr.year = '2012'
UNION
select polr.year, popr.ctyname, popr.POPESTIMATE2013 as
   PopulationCount ,
      polr.Good_Days, polr.Moderate_Days,
        polr.Unhealthy_for_Sensitive_Days, polr.Unhealthy_Days,
          polr.Very_Unhealthy_Days
from polutionanalysisdb.population_raw popr,
   polutionanalysisdb.epaaqi_raw polr
where popr.stname = 'Texas'
and    popr.ctyname like 'Austin%'
and    polr.city_name LIKE 'Austin%'
and    polr.year = '2013'
UNION
select polr.year, popr.ctyname, popr.POPESTIMATE2014 as
```

```
      PopulationCount ,
      polr.Good_Days, polr.Moderate_Days,
        polr.Unhealthy_for_Sensitive_Days, polr.Unhealthy_Days,
          polr.Very_Unhealthy_Days
from polutionanalysisdb.population_raw popr,
  polutionanalysisdb.epaaqi_raw polr
where popr.stname = 'Texas'
and    popr.ctyname like 'Austin%'
and    polr.city_name LIKE 'Austin%'
and    polr.year = '2014'
UNION
select polr.year, popr.ctyname, popr.POPESTIMATE2015 as
  PopulationCount ,
      polr.Good_Days, polr.Moderate_Days,
        polr.Unhealthy_for_Sensitive_Days, polr.Unhealthy_Days,
          polr.Very_Unhealthy_Days
from polutionanalysisdb.population_raw popr,
  polutionanalysisdb.epaaqi_raw polr
where popr.stname = 'Texas'
and    popr.ctyname like 'Austin%'
and    polr.city_name LIKE 'Austin%'
and    polr.year = '2015'
order by 1
```

4. Next, click on **Finish** to save this dataset and then click on **Save & visualize**.

We will now see how to visualize this data.

EPA Trend with population impact

In this section, we will visualize data from the new complex dataset. The first chart that we will create is a simple bar chart with the population trend for Austin over 6 years, as shown here:

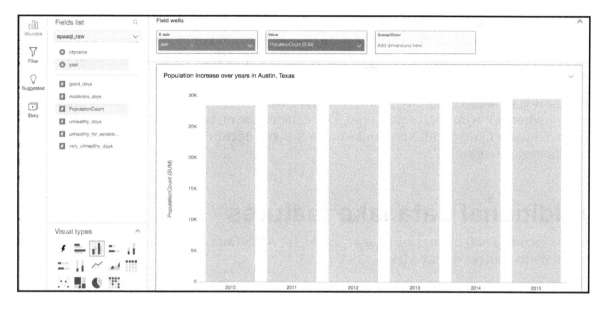

Figure 7.24: EPA and population chart 1

We will create a line chart to show the air quality over time for the same years:

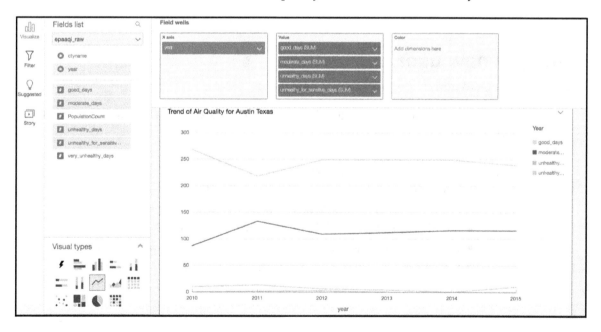

Figure 7.25: EPA and population chart 2

We can see that the increase in population from 2010 to 2015 does seem to have an impact on the air quality index in the city of Austin, Texas. The number of good days has decreased from 268 in 2010 to 239 in 2015; at the same time the population has increased from 28.4 million to 29.5 million.

This now completes our end-to-end AWS Data Lake solution. We built a new AWS Data Lake, hydrated it with source data onto S3, cataloged the metadata, built Athena tables and analyzed using QuickSight. You can leverage this architecture for any other real-life project at your organization.

Additional data lake features

In this section, I will discuss additional features of AWS Data Lake administration that will be handy to manage the data lake.

User management for the AWS Data Lake

The AWS Data Lake solution comes with good user management capabilities that allow administrators to manage access to their users. Let's review the key aspects of user management.

Inviting a new user

Here are the steps to add a new user to our data lake:

1. From the navigation pane, select **Users** under the **Administration** section and then click on **Invite user**.
2. Enter the name, e-mail, and role.
3. A **Member** role has following permissions:
   - View and search for all packages in the data lake
   - Add, remove, and generate manifests for packages
   - Create, update, and delete packages created by them
   - Add and remove datasets from the packages created by them
   - Generate a secret access key if the Administrator has granted them API access

4. An **Admin** role has the following permissions in addition to those that a member has:

- Create user invitations
- Update, disable, enable, and delete data lake users.
- Create, revoke, enable, and disable a user's API access
- Update data lake settings
- Create, update, and delete governance settings

5. Finally, click on **Create Invitation** to send an invitation to the user. The user now has 7 days to sign in to the data lake, after which the invitation expires.

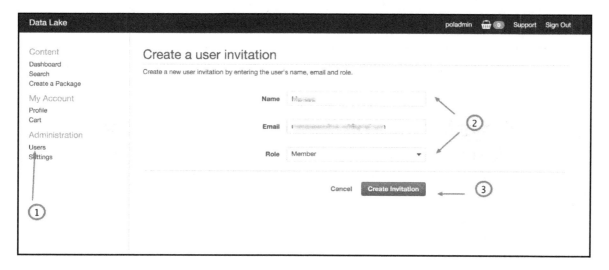

Figure 7.26: Add user

This completes the add user section; next, we will look at updating existing users.

Updating an existing user

If you wish to change the role or details of an existing user, you can follow these steps:

1. From the navigation pane, select **Users** under the **Administration** section and then click on the pencil icon next to the user you want to update.
2. Next, on the **Details** tab, you can modify the role, disable the user, or enable the user.

3. You can also request for an API access key from the **API Access** tab, as shown here:

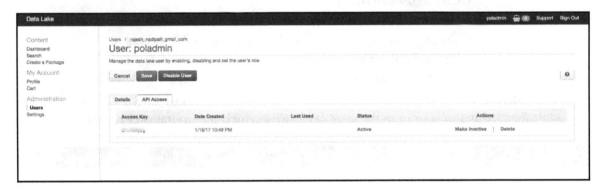

Figure 7.27: User API access

General system settings for AWS Data Lake

To access the data lake settings, click on the **Settings** menu under the **Administration** section from the left navigation pane. I will discuss the key links that this page provides information about:

- **Application Url**: The main URL for the data lake console
- **Default Amazon S3 Bucket**: The S3 bucket used to store datasets and manifests that are uploaded to the data lake
- **Amazon Elasticsearch Index**: The index created for searching packages in the data lake
- **Amazon Elasticsearch Kibana Url**: The URL used for the Kibana application that comes packaged with the data lake
- **Audit Logging**: Enable or disable audit logging. When audit logging is enabled, all user operations within the data lake are logged to the data lake/audit log in the Amazon CloudWatch logs
- **Default Search Results Limit**: The maximum number of hits returned on the user interface when a search is performed. This is also shown here:

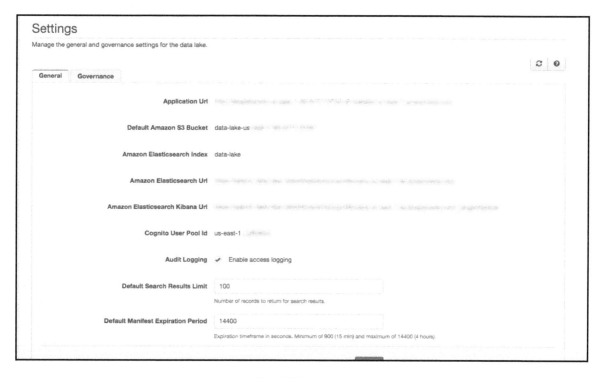

Figure 7.28: General settings

Summary

Data lake is the popular way to store and analyze data as it has the promise of storing any data in a central location and serving multiple business needs. In this chapter, we looked at how the various services that Amazon has put together in AWS Data Lake solution truly accelerate the build-out of such a data lake. The AWS Data Lake comes packaged with a reference implementation and a complete web application for governing the metadata, thereby allowing data stewards to publish and data consumers to search and extract from the data lake. We also saw how QuickSight is a core component of this solution and provides insights into the data.

In the final chapter, I will review some exciting features coming with the QuickSight product that will make it easier for integration and adoption.

8
QuickSight Product Shortcomings

QuickSight is a new AWS service and was launched in November 2016. While the product is revolutionary and has a bold vision, there are several shortcomings with the current version for it to replace enterprise BI solutions. In this chapter, we will review the following:

- A recap of the key product features
- Features lacking and what is in the roadmap
- User guide and community forum

QuickSight product features

QuickSight is designed to make analysis easy for all employees within an organization – with interactive visualizations, ad hoc analysis, and the ability to query data from most AWS data sources. Let's review the key features of the product; I have grouped them into the following categories:

- Visualizations and ad hoc analysis
- Data connectivity
- Data preparation
- Sharing and access
- User management
- Operations

Easy ad hoc analysis and visualizations

QuickSight's primary objective is to provide cloud-powered business analytics as a service for everyday analysis. Here are the key features in this category:

- **Ease of use**: QuickSight empowers people from all roles in an organization to easily explore their data from any source and visualization for your data without any IT involvement
- **Wide variety of visualizations**: QuickSight supports bar charts, line graphs, area line charts, scatter plots, heat maps, pie graphs, tree maps, and pivot tables
- **Smart visualizations**: QuickSight comes with an autograph feature that automatically infers data type and provides suggestions for best possible visualizations

The following screenshot shows a QuickSight dashboard, which is a convenient way to share an analysis with others:

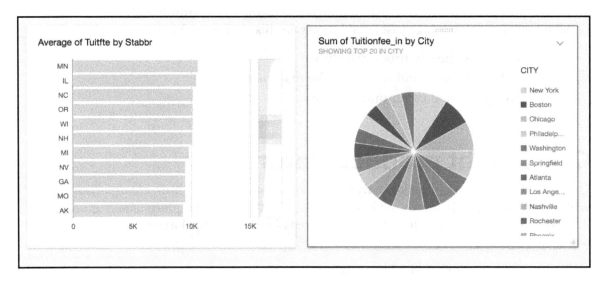

Figure 8.1: QuickSight visuals

Wide range of data connectivity

In this section, we will review QuickSight's features for data connectivity:

- **Deep integration with AWS sources**: QuickSight can connect to several AWS data sources, including EMR, RDS, DynamoDB, Redshift, Kinesis, Athena, and S3. QuickSight seamlessly discovers the data sources that are available in your account.
- **Self service ingestion**: QuickSight allows you to upload your data using Excel, CSV, TSV, CLF, and ELF. You can also import data from SaaS applications such as Salesforce.
- **Source from on-premises databases**: QuickSight can connect to on-premises databases such as SQL Server, MySQL, and PostgreSQL.

The following screenshot shows different data sources supported by the current version of QuickSight:

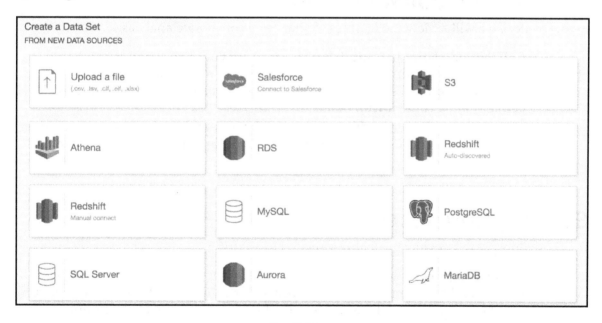

Figure 8.2: Datasets

Fast and visual data preparation

For scenarios where your data is not clean and/or needs to be joined with reference data before it is used, QuickSight can help. Let's review these data preparation features:

- **Functions**: QuickSight supports various functions to format and transform your data. You can change data types and use one of many string, date, numeric, and conditional functions before it is visualized.
- **Joins**: QuickSight also supports join operations using a simple drag and drop interface.
- **Blazing fast performance**: QuickSight is powered by SPICE, a super fast calculation engine that delivers unprecedented performance of these transformations at big data scale as it caches data in memory in distributed mode.

Sharing and collaboration

In this section, we will review the features to share and collaborate analysis:

- **Collaborate, share, and publish**: You can share your live analyses, read-only dashboards, and storyboards with any number of recipients using e-mail addresses, usernames, or a group name. You can also control the permission level before sharing content with others.
- **Mobile and web access**: All analyses, dashboards, and stories can be accessed on any device supporting a web browser and native applications for iPads and iPhones.

Security and access

In this section, we will review the features related to security:

- **User management**: You can manage up to 100 user accounts in the standard edition, and an unlimited number if you go for enterprise edition AD accounts. Users can be added with just an e-mail address or using the IAM account.
- **Managing QuickSight access**: You can control the permissions given to QuickSight to access your AWS resources with an account that has QuickSight administration privileges.

The following screenshot shows how to manage access to QuickSight from the various data sources:

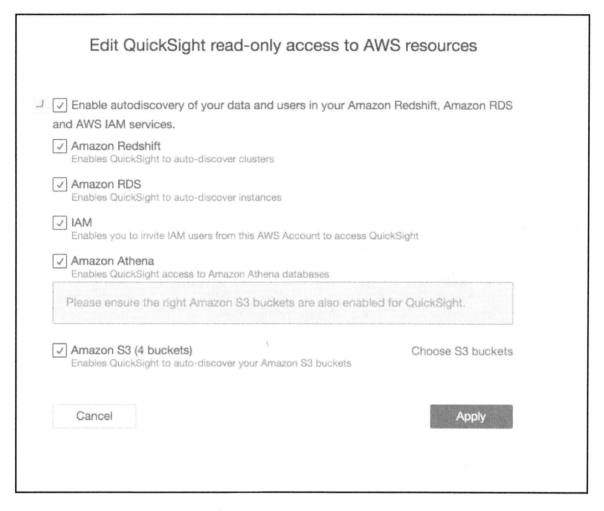

Figure 8.3: Security and access

Easy operations

QuickSight is a fully managed cloud BI service with no hardware or software to license. Let's review the key features related to hosting and operations:

- **Cost effective**: QuickSight is priced at $9 per user per month (for the Standard edition) and is a complete managed service which eliminates the need for software installation and maintenance. The following table provides details on pricing and tiers:

	Free tier	Standard edition	Enterprise edition
Price per user per month	$0	$9 (annual commitment) / $12 (no commitment)	$18 (annual commitment) / $24 (no commitment)
SPICE capacity (GB/user)	1 GB	10 GB	10 GB
Additional GB cost per month	$0.25	$0.25	$0.38

- **Zero infrastructure management**: QuickSight just requires a web browser and also works great on mobile devices. It does not require any hardware or software to manage and does not require additional licenses.

That completes the high-level feature overview of AWS QuickSight; next we will look into what features it lacks.

Features lacking in QuickSight

Okay, now let's get a reality check with the product and see which features it is either lacking or needs significant enhancement, so that it can be considered a viable enterprise BI tool replacement.

In the next few pages, I will group these features in categories and also indicate which of these features are already in the product roadmap.

Lack of integration with the visualization layer

The following are the features that I expect will be added to the product for integrations:

- **Integrations with SPICE (in roadmap)**: SPICE is what makes QuickSight really fast and is designed to run interactive queries on large datasets in memory. SPICE is currently only being used by QuickSight visualizations and the product management team has mentioned that external applications such as Tableau, DOMO, and Qlik will be able to integrate with this layer, making the QuickSight value proposition really higher. It is also suggested that SPICE will have a SQL-like access provided for additional third-party applications via APIs and/or an ODBC connector.

- **Embedding visuals to other websites (in roadmap)**: If you, as a user, like the reports generated by QuickSight, you might need the ability to embed it on a custom website. This feature should support passing variables as parameters to the dashboard to make this integration easier to use.

Only basic visualizations

The following are the features that I expect will be added to the product for the category of visualizations and analysis:

- **Clone existing analysis**: Often, you may wish to preserve an existing analysis and create, and then modify, a new one based on it.

- **Advanced charting**: The charting options provided by QuickSight do support the commonly used scenarios, but there are several other types that enterprise BI applications have that are missing. The following are a few:
    - Geospatial heatmaps (in roadmap)
    - Gantt chart
    - Histogram chart
    - Filled maps (colors based on a metric on a region/country)
    - Box-and-whisker plot
    - Regression analysis

- **Source code management**: To promote code from one environment, such as development to production, we need the ability to check-in and check-out the analysis and dashboard definitions to a Git or SVN repository.

- **Site branding (in roadmap)**: QuickSight currently does not allow users to customize the look and feel to suite their custom corporate needs like a logo and custom CSS.
- **Usability**: QuickSight needs improvement in managing filters, legends, and its ability to add text to analysis.

This completes the feature gaps in visualizations and analysis; next, we will review the gaps in sharing and collaboration.

Limited mobile and sharing

In this section we will review the features lacking in the sharing and collaboration category:

- **Mobile support for android devices (in roadmap)**: Currently mobile support is limited to Apple devices and I expect the android native app to be released soon
- **Download data and charts (in roadmap)**: From the analysis and dashboard pages, there is no option to download the data and/or visuals to Excel or PDF for offline analysis and sharing
- **Usability**: With dashboard feature, the product needs improvement in managing filters, adding text, and images, to make it more effective

Lack of advanced data management

The following are features that I expect will be added to the product for the category of data management:

- **Integration with DynamoDB (in roadmap)**: DynamoDB is a popular NoSQL database service provided by AWS and currently there is no integration with QuickSight.
- **Hierarchy support**: QuickSight charts do support drill down so that we can go from a higher level of metrics like state level to a child level like city. This hierarchy management is not easy to use and is useful in several types of dashboards/metrics reporting.
- **Organizing the catalog**: Currently, the list of existing data sources is shown under the **Manage data** section. This list is a simple tile view with three data sources shown per line ordered by last used on top. This should be better organized by category and importance by the end user. Additionally, each tile should show a quick stat like total number of records and size of the source.

The following screenshot shows the current catalog which simply orders all data sets in descending order of creation:

Figure 8.4: Data sets not organized

Advanced data preparation features

Let's review the data preparation features that QuickSight is lacking:

- **Operations pipeline**: When you revisit a data set which had a series or data preparation steps, it is not clear as to what changes were made and in what sequence. Other BI tools typically show the list of operations either as steps or visually as a pipeline.
- **Lineage**: QuickSight supports joins and functions which alter the original data. For compliance and audits, it is necessary to have a lineage report to show where the data came from along with all the operations done on it at every field level. This lineage feature does not exist today.

Lack of fine grain access

In this section, we will review the features lacking related to security:

- **Governance (in roadmap)**: QuickSight has plans to add governance to data sets so that an administrator can manage who gets access to which data sets
- **Fine grain access control (in roadmap)**: QuickSight does not have the ability to restrict certain portions of data to specific individuals; for example, for compliance needs customers often want to grant access to sensitive data to only certain individuals of the organization

General

Here are some other general features that QuickSight lacks:

- **Error logging**: QuickSight server side logs are not accessible even with administration role. This would be useful in troubleshooting issues that cannot be resolved on the user interface.
- **Audit logs (in roadmap)**: Currently there is no easy way to track who accessed what data using QuickSight.

Accessing the user guide

QuickSight has a detailed user guide that is accessible from the right-hand side corner under the user icon as shown in the following screenshot:

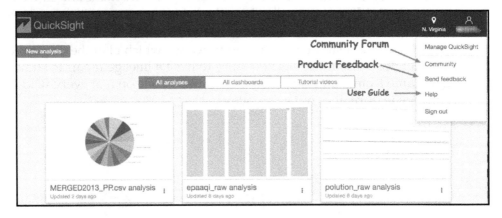

Figure 8.5: User guide and feedback

The help can also be accessed using this URL
`http://docs.aws.amazon.com/quicksight/latest/user/welcome.html`.

The user guide is organized by various categories as seen in the following screenshot:

Figure 8.6: QuickSight help

Providing feedback

QuickSight has two ways for you to provide feedback:

- First, is a feedback link that sends an e-mail to the QuickSight product development team.
- Second, is a community forum where you can also search for responses from others using the product The community forum is pretty useful with quick search, and popular tags that can narrow results. You can also ask a new question to the forum and post a new idea. If your idea is good, you will get others to vote for you, and the QuickSight product management team is constantly reviewing this forum.

The following screenshot highlights the links to forums and search:

Figure 8.7: Community forum

Summary

QuickSight is a cloud-native business analytics service that is poised to disrupt the traditional BI tools and will empower users to explore and visualize data on their own, without the need for long IT cycles. QuickSight product features can be categorized under the following groups: easy visualization, wide data connectivity, visual data preparation, sharing and security. While QuickSight delivers on theses core feature sets, there are several feature gaps when compared to an enterprise product, primarily in regard to usability, integrations, and visualizations.

QuickSight is owned by the largest cloud hosting company in the world and is strategically important for the AWS Data Lake Solution, which means that Amazon will most likely add several features or acquire related software to improve their client experience in the year 2017. I encourage readers to get involved by providing valuable feedback to AWS using QuickSight forums to help make this product better for all. Happy analytics!!!

Index

www.ingramcontent.com/pod-product-compliance
Lightning Source LLC
Chambersburg PA
CBHW060536060326
40690CB00017B/3510